YESTERDAY TODAY *tomorrow*
TRAGEDY DOESN'T DEFINE YOU

COL MACKERETH

Published by Change Empire Books
www.changeempire.com

All rights reserved

Printed on demand in Australia, United States and United Kingdom

Edited & designed by Change Empire Books

This book is sold subject to the condition that it shall not, by way of trade or otherwise, be lent, resold, hired out, or otherwise circulated without the publisher's prior consent in any form of binding or cover other than that in which it is published and without a similar condition including this condition being imposed on the subsequent purchaser.

The scanning, uploading, and distribution of this book via the internet or via any other means without the permission of the publisher is illegal and punishable by law. Please purchase only authorised electronic editions and do not participate in or encourage electronic piracy of copyrightable materials. Your support of the authors' rights is appreciated.

While the authors have made every effort to provide accurate internet addresses at the time of publication, neither the publisher nor the authors assume any responsibility for errors or for changes that occur after publication. Furthermore, the publisher does not have any control over and does not assume any responsibility for author or third-party websites or their content.

EBOOK ISBN: 978-0-6488138-1-1

PRINT ISBN: 978-0-6488138-2-8

DEDICATION

To the girl who spun the bottle, the classmate who didn't go to the reunion, and the woman who proposed.

CONTENTS

THE LIVED EXPERIENCE — 13

1	A Sliding Door	15
2	Lost Dreams	25
3	Blood, Sweat and Tears	35
4	One of the Boys	47
5	The Great Aussie Dream	59
6	Sex, Drugs, and Rock 'n' Roll	67
7	On the Farm	77
8	Life and Death	91
9	Living the Dream	103
10	Something's Missing	111
11	Soulmates	121
12	Sharing the Lived Experience	133
13	Agents of Change	141

THE 8 KEYS — 147

14	Identity	151
15	Thought Power	157
16	Visualisation	165
17	Belief	171
18	Self-Worth	177
19	Comfort Zones	185
20	Self-Talk	193
21	Ownership	201

FOREWORD

Those of us who have experienced an unfortunate trauma and life-changing spinal cord injury, in particular a high cervical one, sometimes feel like we belong to a gang or fraternity – a pack. We're a pretty recognisable crew, especially to each other. It might be the four halo traction scars around our heads, the contracted, curled over fingers, the posture while sitting in our wheelchairs, or even the prevalent "quad gut." It's not uncommon for me to be rolling down the street and spot another wheelie up ahead. We'll pass by one another and give a nod of acknowledgment, a sign of understanding of what each other has experienced to bring ourselves to this place, with this condition, in these wheelchairs.

Sometimes it's more than a nod. It's a greeting, followed by some deeper conversation about our injuries: how it happened, when and where. And while there will always be some slight variations, a lot of the post-accident and rehabilitation memories have many similarities. This is why we feel like we belong in the gang. We can relate to each other, and we connect.

Some connections are strong from first contact. This was Col and I. Unlike our damaged spinal cords, our friendship and work relationship have always had a strong current of communication. We've talked a lot about life in general, but most of our discussions are based around life with a disability and spinal cord injury experiences. We share resources and information about everything from travel to work, equipment to medications, clothes modifications to quadriplegic-friendly shaving techniques. Nothing's out of bounds. We lay it all out there because we know each other; we've wheeled a similar path and we're heading in a similar direction.

Since my own spinal cord injury in 1999, there have been three people with quadriplegia who have become like older brothers to me. Col is one. These men have helped mould the man I am today. They are people with an incredible zest for life. They have continued to follow their dreams, no matter what obstacle lay in front of them. They have achieved success by motivating themselves to get the most out of their bodies and their minds and, in turn, have inspired others to follow suit, including myself.

Col's life was turned upside-down in 1978, and instead of sitting in his chair, halting his dreams, and complaining about the cards he'd been dealt, he learned through necessity how to keep moving. How to keep striving for the goals he set in his life. Though many trials and tribulations still await him on his journey, Col has unlocked the keys to his potential and pathways to success. He leads by example, and his life and achievements to date are a testament to his strong will, passion for learning, and eagerness for forward movement and action.

We may be connected, albeit via similar disabilities, but it's Col's attitude that I am drawn to the most. I want to be in his gang. I want to wheel in the same direction of life success with someone like Col beside me.

Yesterday Today Tomorrow is his story, and may it inspire and motivate you in a way you've never experienced before. The exploration and discovery of new abilities in our lives is a remarkable thing, and through Col's own life experiences, he has now produced a practical model and template to follow, interspersed with some great yarns and emotional life commentary.

Thanks, Col.

Tim McCallum
(your little brother in arms)

PREFACE

It doesn't matter what you want to change in your life; it's easy once you know how to think effectively.

Once I learned I can change my current situation just by the way I think, a whole new world of opportunities opened up for me.

Now it's time to share my secrets with you.

Yesterday Today Tomorrow will give you insight into how I survived and thrived after my spinal cord injury. It will help you to think in a way that can change your old habits and build your new lifestyle.

In Part One, I'll share with you my lived experiences of the last 41 years, living with a spinal cord injury.

The highlights.

The lowlights.

The in-between lights.

I'll share with you the lessons I've learned along the way.

You'll probably laugh.

You'll probably cry, too.

But you definitely won't be bored.

You may even be inspired and motivated.

I've been to places I never thought I would be able to go.

I've achieved goals I never would have even considered setting.

In Part Two, I'll share with you how my current thoughts and my self-talk have made that possible, even under the tragic circumstances I was dealt.

I'll share with you my 8 keys to meaningful and sustainable change.

INTRODUCTION

It's hard to imagine how you would react if you were tragically struck down in your youth.

And why would you? It's not like anything like that is ever going to happen.

I was 10 feet tall and bullet-proof. Nothing could possibly knock me down. Even if it did, I'd get straight back up again.

It's hard to imagine how your world can be shattered into pieces in an instant. Everything you ever dreamed of, stolen by one careless action.

Replaced with a nightmare of uncertainty without any chance of resurrection. A life without a light at the end of the tunnel.

It's hard to imagine how you could possibly pick up the pieces of your old life or even try to build a new one.

But, nevertheless, pick up the pieces I did.

Unfortunately, once you're in this situation, you don't really have a choice. Well, I guess you could just roll over and give up, but that's not the way I roll. That's the worst pun you'll read in this book. I promise.

Irrespective of whether we've experienced a life-changing trauma or not, most of us are on a journey or a quest to be the best version of "us" we can be. We just want to grow, learn, and continually improve our lifestyle.

Many of us have something that we want to change about ourselves. It may be a habit, a personality trait, a state of mind, or something about our lifestyles.

Some of us are trying to get out of an undesirable situation at work or in a relationship; sometimes we're just looking for a sea change.

Some want to become successful (whatever that means). Some want to find true love. Some just want to be happy.

It's rare to find someone who is completely happy with every aspect of their lives.

There is usually some imbalance, but often when we make changes to one aspect of our lives there is a trade-off in another area, and before long we find ourselves back where we started.

Many of us have tried to make changes in our lives without success. Some of us have tried many, many times and failed.

Unless we approach change in the right way, we usually find that we just end up back where we started.

All of your answers might not be in this book, but I'm sure it will point you in the right direction.

PART ONE

THE LIVED EXPERIENCE

CHAPTER 1
A SLIDING DOOR

"Get off me you ugly bastard," I thought, too short of breath to say the words out loud and unable to move my arms to push him away.

Johnny Beare was pinching my nose with his left hand and holding my chin with his right as he leaned in, open mouthed, about to kiss me full on the lips. Then the penny dropped – he wasn't trying to kiss me, he was trying to save my life.

Why on earth would I be needing mouth to mouth? … and why would it be him and not one of the girls?

It was then that the events leading up to this moment began to emerge from the haze in my head.

As I lay on the creek bank, with a weird "pins and needles" sensation washing all over my body, I recalled how the day had started.

I had woken that glorious spring morning to the high-pitched screams of a bunch of 7-year-old girls excited to be celebrating my baby sister Katrina's birthday. It was Sunday, 24 September 1978.

Celebrating! I'd done my fair share of celebrating the night before at the White Horse Tavern. I had not long since turned 18 and was still tickled by the concept of legally drinking in a pub.

As I dragged my hungover arse out of bed and staggered up the back stairs to the bathroom, I glanced up at the clock on Mum's fridge. "Fuck me! It's 10:30!"

There was no way I could get a lift to the Foley Shield Rugby League Carnival in Townsville now. Everyone who was going would be long gone by now.

My head was banging, my mouth was dry, and it tasted like I'd licked every ashtray at the Tavern. Combined with the joyful squeals coming from the birthday party, there was no way I could have stayed at home.

Just when I thought my only sensible option was to go back to the pub, my mate Johnny Beare dropped by with his girlfriend, Karen and two of her boarding school friends.

"You wanna come out to the Fletcher with us for a swim?"

My shittiest day of the year just took a turn for the better. Lying in Fletcher Creek was one of the best hangover cures known to man.

After the briefest of introductions, I was in the middle of the back seat of the Holden Gemini, puffing my chest out and doing my best to impress the beautiful creatures on either side.

My courtship performance ramped up as we arrived at the creek. Without saying a word, I jumped out of the car, ran down to the water's edge and executed an almost perfect "dead soldier dive" into the crisp, cool water.

BANG!!

My head exploded into a million stars, as though I'd just been struck by a bolt of lightning. A weird tingling sensation shot up and down my spine and a buzzing hum like high voltage power lines rang in my ears.

The water didn't feel cold like I'd expected it to. It didn't even feel wet. But I could taste the unmistakable metallic, basalt tinge unique to the Fletcher.

As I floated down the creek face down, I could see my arms hanging limp in front of me. It was like they weren't even my arms…but whose arms could they be? As my lifeless fingers dragged through the sand of the creek bed, I could pick up the faint tinkle of the grains of sand as they tumbled along in the current.

This time of year, before the start of the wet season, the Fletcher was barely knee deep. I knew that before I dived. Hell, I'd only ever been to this spot a hundred times before.

"You never dive into the Fletcher, mate." Dad had told me this from the time I was big enough to hold a fishing rod. "The water's so crystal clear it's hard to tell just how deep it is."

My "dead soldier dive" was looking perfect so far, but my playing dead routine didn't have anyone fooled…and consequently nobody really worried about me for quite a while.

I tried and tried to raise my head out of the water, but not even my neck muscles responded. I only managed to make little bobbing movements, which only added to my act. At that point, I started to worry I was going to drown before one of the girls would come running to my rescue. I'd grab her and wrestle her into the water beside me and shout "Gotcha!" She'd giggle, I'd laugh, and somehow our lips would meet…

Then everything went black.

That's when the nightmare started.

All of a sudden, the girl in my vision was gone and it was Johnny's open mouth moving in on me.

This was not how I'd pictured my day going at all.

"I'm fine, I'm fine," I spluttered. "I just need to catch my breath." I'd had a similar sensation another time, years ago. I'd jumped stiff-legged into what I thought was quicksand, only to find it wasn't. After taking a minute to catch my breath, I made a full recovery. Today would surely be no different.

"Can you feel this?" Karen asked in a calm tone that masked her concern.

"Feel what?" I was confused

"This? I'm touching your leg." There was a hint of realisation now in her voice as she touched my leg again.

"You're not touching my leg," I said, still not fully comprehending what was going on.

Suddenly the mood changed. The colour drained out of their faces as they realised the severity of my situation.

I was still in denial, waiting to catch my breath and get back in the water.

"I'm going into town to get the ambulance," Johnny said. There was no other way to call them, not in 1978.

"No, don't do that," I insisted. "If you think it's that bad, then you better take me back to town." An ambulance would have taken forever to get out there. It was at least a 30-minute trip each way.

By this time shock had set in, and I was only conscious of a few brief moments over the next few hours.

As we drove back to town, me in the front seat – this time with one of the girls holding my head straight from behind – I became aware of unusual sensations in weird parts of my body.

I could feel my face blushing with embarrassment from the reflex erection bulging through my shorts, stimulated by the near-death experience I'd just had. "God," I thought, "I hope she doesn't notice that."

I knew when we'd arrived at the Charters Towers Base Hospital. The smell of the pencil pine trees had always haunted me as a child.

Matron Helen Pansini stood beside the car, ripping Johnny a new arsehole. "You idiot! We'll have to call the ambulance to come and cut him out with the jaws of life!"

"Hang on a minute," I tried to say, "this bloke just saved my life!" But my words didn't have any sound, and her rant faded into the blackness.

Some time later, I found myself lying on my back, fully naked, in the emergency treatment room.

"Nurse," someone said, "cut those shorts off and clean him up so that I can catheterise him." The nurse jumped, as they usually did when matron barked an order.

I couldn't tell if I still had an erection or not. My erratic thoughts were focused on the demise of my favourite pair of shorts.

"No, not my blue shorts," I tried to protest. The small, tight shorts would have made Warwick Kappa's look like pyjama bottoms. "You better not throw them out, Mum should be able to fix them up."

I missed the ambulance trip to Townsville and the plane ride from there to Brisbane. I must have drifted off for a bit longer this time.

"G'day mate, my name's Andrew, Andrew Perrin." The voice came from a young man beside me, lying flat in a frightful contraption I later found out was an Edgerton bed, his head in traction. He had stainless steel tongs driven into either side of his skull, with what looked like dried blood running down behind his ears. A bag of sand hung off it, connected by a rope.

I didn't hear him. Well, not consciously, anyway.

"What's this big dopey ringer think he's doing?" I yelled. "Shit stirring and looking for a blue! I'll fucking sort his shit out! You got my back, mate?"

"Col, it's me, Mum." Mum was sitting beside my bed, holding my hand. "There's no one else here, love. You're in hospital in Brisbane." Mum could always calm me down.

"If this prick wants a blue, I'm just the man he's looking for! Hold my money, I'm going to sort this bastard out!"

"You haven't got any money, love." Mum stroked my hand, unable to settle me this time.

"Look in my hand! What's that? A lump of cow shit? There's 50 cent coins all through this bed and it feels like a dollar note shoved up my arse!"

Mum lifted my hand up in front of my eyes to show me it was empty.

That scene ended abruptly and another random situation started to play out in my head.

"Mum! I've got to stop these biros coming out of my nostrils!" As fast as I pulled one out, another one appeared. It was like a magician pulling coloured hankies out of his fist.

Reality and delirium danced together hideously in the ballroom of my brain for all of the first week and most of the next. Delirium took the lead.

Pethidine often has a hallucinatory effect, but at least I wasn't in any pain.

As sanity regained control, I began to become aware of my surroundings and the young bloke in the bed beside me.

"What did you say your name was again, mate?" I asked.

"Andrew Perrin," he said

"Andrew Perrin." I repeated, and then said again, to myself, "Andrew Perrin? I know this bloke," I thought. "Yes… OH FUCK YES!" I finally remembered. It was just the other day back in Cloncurry, and it came back to me as clear as if it were today.

I had walked from the Main Roads Department (MRD) office, where I'd just started my drafting cadetship, to the single men's quarters, picked up my footy boots, and gone to the oval. By this time, most of the Tigers players had already arrived. Strangely, though, none of them had started the mandatory warm-up laps; they were all just standing around. There was none of the usual banter and carry-on; everybody was deadly serious.

"Bit early in the week to be hung over, isn't it?" I sat down and started to lace up my boots.

"You haven't heard, then?" Buster said. "Young Andrew Perrin got smashed up on Sunday."

"They're a bunch of grubs, those Julia Creek pricks," I said. "I hope his forwards give 'em some back."

"No, mate, they had to stop the game. His neck's broke. He's in hospital in Brisbane, paralysed, can't move anything but his eyeballs."

"FUCK, REALLY?" I said, thinking, "The poor bastard. I'd top myself if that happened to me."

Yeah, I knew him all right. I hadn't ever met him in person, but I knew who he was. A bloody good little footballer, too, but one who would never play again.

"You didn't make it to the Foley Shield either, then, mate." I stated the obvious. We had common ground.

"No," Andrew replied. "Doesn't look like either of us will be playing for a while. Doctors told me I'd be in traction for 10–12 weeks."

The Edgerton bed that I found myself lying in was specifically designed for patients with acute cervical spinal injuries. I too had skull tongs inserted; 15 pounds of traction kept my neck in alignment and perfectly still while the vertebrae healed. The red stuff I'd thought was blood on Andrew's head was a gauze dressing soaked in mercurochrome. It stung like a bitch every time it got changed.

We had fractured the same vertebrae in our necks and damaged our spinal cords.

Two strong young blokes from the bush, both now completely paralysed from the shoulders down.

Two young footballers unable to move anything but their eyeballs, supposedly.

"Well, the boys back in the 'Curry got that one wrong," I thought.

C6 Quadriplegia – or, to use the preferred medical term, "C6 Tetraplegia" – was our official diagnosis.

Nobody ever used either of those terms. We were generally just referred to as "quads."

With this level of spinal injury, it was expected that we would only regain the use of some muscles in our upper arms – shoulders, biceps, wrist extension – but only time would tell if we would get any more.

Like the boys back in the 'Curry, I had always thought that if you were a quadriplegic, a "quad," you couldn't move anything but your eyeballs. My aunty Pat had always told us to "be careful or you might break your neck and die" whenever we took unnecessary risks.

Well, I didn't die, and neither did Andrew. I guess that's gotta be a good thing.

Andrew and I seemed to have identical injuries with identical prognosis. We were both about to embark on identical journeys of recovery. The only difference was that he would always be a couple of weeks ahead.

"Time for your turn!" The loud Scottish voice boomed through the room as Bob the wardie snatched the curtain back and turned on the lights. In the bright light I couldn't make out his face, but I could see the smoke wafting up from the cigarette stuck in the corner of his lips. A half inch of ash was about to fall off onto my bed. I caught the sweet smell of my favourite tobacco, Champion Ruby, and instantly I was craving a cigarette.

I hadn't known what time it was or even if it was night or day since being admitted almost a fortnight before, and I hadn't had a smoke in that long, either.

Bob had a team of nurses and another wardie with him. The nurses took care of my head traction while the other wardie adjusted the side rail on the bed. Bob carefully pressed his foot on the pedal which controlled the Edgerton bed. The bed's electric motors whirred into action and the bed slowly turned onto its side.

"Good to see you back with the land of the living," he said. "You've been driving everyone crazy with all your screaming and nonsense."

"We thought they were going to come over from next door and cart you off in a straightjacket." A brand-new psych unit had just been opened by Premier Bjelke Peterson beside the spinal unit.

"I'd kill for a smoke," I said, not minding that I was begging.

"I'm sure if you ask nicely, one of these lovely ladies will sort that out for you," he said, dodging having to fork out one of his own.

While I lay on my side, the nurses rubbed my back and heels to get the circulation going again and relieve pressure which might cause bed sores. Not that I could feel it. They changed the sheets, the kerosene smell of freshly laundered hospital sheets mixed with the lingering whiffs of Bob's cigarette.

One of the nurses did come back later in the evening to share a smoke with me. We didn't talk. I just lay there in the darkness, trying to take in what had been going on over the previous fortnight.

We were turned in the Edgerton beds regularly. Four hours on the back, two hours on the side, four hours on the back, two hours on the other side.

Day and night. Night and day.

Four hours on my back, two hours on my side, four hours on my back, two hours on my side – without fail for the next ten weeks.

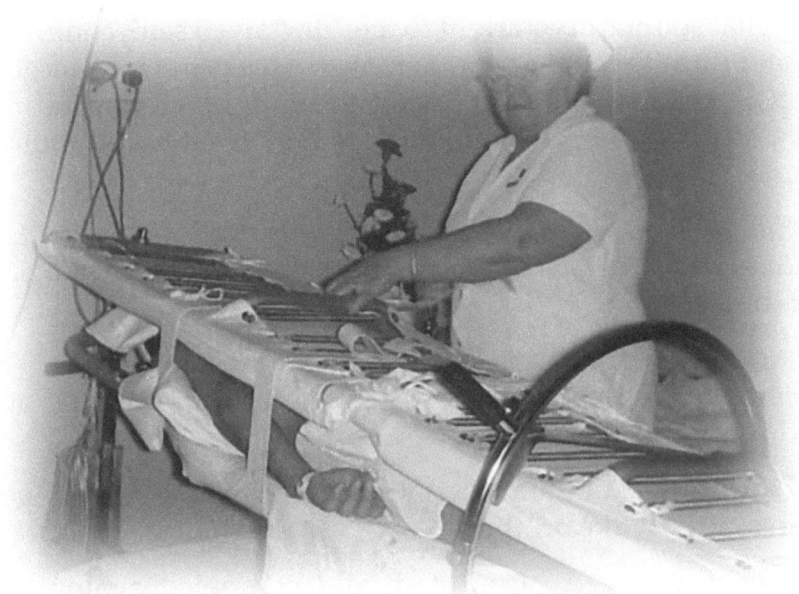

CHAPTER 2
LOST DREAMS

I couldn't remember ever being in hospital for more than a night in my whole life. I'd never broken a bone or even had a stitch before this.

"Andrew reckons I'll be stuck in bed for ten more weeks. That can't be right, can it?" I asked Bronwen, the second-year nurse. You could tell the nurses' rank by the stripes on their hats. All the sisters, or registered nurses, as they're now known, wore huge "flying nun" hats and had blue lapels on their shoulders.

Sister Pollock was in charge. She had red lapels. Just like Matron Pansini, everyone jumped when she issued a command.

"That sounds about right to me," Bronwen said, confirming what I didn't want to hear. Ten more weeks in bed was going to be a challenge. I didn't want to think much beyond that, let alone how long after that before I'd be better and could go home.

Surely that's not right? Surely I'll be better soon and get home in time for the footy grand final. The Tigers were undefeated so far this season.

Andrew's family and mine visited almost every day. They became quite close and were a great support for each other and for us.

During that time in traction, Andrew and I became good mates, almost like brothers. We developed a brotherly rivalry.

We encouraged, supported, and competed against each other in almost everything we did. Sometimes we'd even get the nurses to move our beds close together so we could arm wrestle and try and pull each other out of bed. We were in this together. Neither of us got an early release from our shackles.

I had lots of visitors, especially in the early weeks. Some of my Tigers footy mates even came to visit all the way from Cloncurry.

My skull tongs had Chook a bit confused. He took one look at them and asked me with a frown on his face, "Does that thing go right through the middle of your brain?" He wasn't the sharpest tool in the shed.

"No, mate, just into the skull." It wouldn't be the last time I had to answer that question, either.

Chook wasn't much of a diplomat, either, and said bluntly, "It's gotta suck you'll never play footy again."

That was the first time it struck me I would never play footy again, much less walk again, not that any of the doctors ever said those words exactly.

They didn't have to.

Deep down I knew, but I wasn't ready to admit it. What was the hurry? I had ten more weeks of head traction to look forward to before I needed to worry about footy.

Ten more weeks of Edgerton bed turns every few hours.

I didn't know then that not being able to walk was only the tip of the iceberg.

I didn't know I would never piss again without using a catheter.

I didn't know I wouldn't have control over my bowels and would shit my pants on a regular basis.

I didn't know I would never be able to regulate my own body temperature again.

I didn't know I would have uncontrollable muscle spasms and constant neuropathic pain 24 hours a day for the rest of my life.

If a magic genie jumped out of a lamp today and said, "I have the power to let you walk again," I'd probably ask if I could swap for "piss without a catheter."

I had so much ahead of me and so much to learn. We all did.

The spinal unit at the Princess Alexandra Hospital was a busy unit specifically for people with spinal injuries. Forty-four beds, always full of people just like me and Andrew. Young blokes in their teens to twenties. Mostly car or bike accidents or sporting injuries, with a few seasonal divers like myself.

Ninety new patients every year. Ninety promising futures turned upside down.

The class of '78–'79 was a melting pot of people from all different walks of life. All different backgrounds and lifestyles.

Malcom "Stud" Perry, a quad from Dalby, broke his neck in a glider crash. Stud was in charge of allocating the nicknames, and yes, he gave himself that name. While I would go on to share a flat with Stud, I'd never understand why that name was fitting.

"Froggie" was a 19-year-old Frenchman. He could only speak a dozen words in English. As it turned out, he would go on to regain the use of his frog's legs and be able to stand unassisted, but still have little use of his hands or fingers. Froggie was a diver just like me, although I doubt his dive was anywhere near as spectacular as mine.

"Slug," a 16-year-old para, took to the wheelchair as if he were born in it. He didn't have an accident; he had a tumour removed from his spine. As for his nickname, I never shared a shower with him so I can neither confirm nor deny the resemblance.

Then there was Tommy "Triangle" – nobody could pronounce his last name; it was Tri-something. Another 16-year-old motorbike crash para. Every morning, he stole a pen from one of the nurses and wrote "I HATE SKOOL" in four different colours on his sheets.

Bill was an industrial chemist who would go on to become a professor at uni and teach chemistry to a generation of up and coming chemists. Bill was the quad that we all thought of before our injuries. He was completely paralysed from the neck down and never regained anything. Not too sure why he never got a nickname. He was hit by a car while riding a push bike.

Ruark didn't get a nickname, either. Who needed one with a name like Ruark? That's probably not how it's spelled, but I didn't have a lot to do with him. He spent most of his time smoking hash oil and speaking in strange tongues. Car crash.

Gordon was 28 but looked about 40. He was christened "Fossil" (because Stud thought he looked like one). Crashed a motorbike and lay in a ditch for hours. His spinal damage was caused from blood loss to his spinal cord, not from a fracture.

Everyone had their own story of where they'd come from and how they got here. Everyone was on their own journey of recovery and rehabilitation.

But everywhere you go, there's always the one!

The one was George "Cookie" Cook, another Stud classic original nickname. Cookie was the king of the ward, a T12 para from a car crash. Cookie was the lovable larrikin, always looking for ways to make mischief. I'm guessing he'd always been that way even prior to his accident.

"Good morning, Colin," Cookie would say, trying to sound posh, his infectious two-tooth smile beaming out from under his ginger Merv Hughes moustache. I could almost smell his sweaty armpits and cigarette-and-beer breath before I heard his raspy, high-pitched voice.

"No, not this morning," I'd plead. "Please, not this morning."

He would come past my bed early every morning on his way to the communal bathrooms. Lighting two cigarettes, he'd stick one between my toes and the other in his mouth and then disappear.

"Get back here, you prick," I'd call. "Take it out, you bastard!"

I was like a beached turtle, lying on my back and watching the smouldering cigarette through my prism glasses, unable to do anything about it.

"Nurse! Nurse!" I'd scream, only about a third of my lung capacity working. The chances of a nurse coming at that time of day were slim, even if they could hear me down at the nurses' station.

"You're such a sookie la la cry baby," Cookie would laugh when he returned from his smoke, and that's exactly how I felt. Like a baby, useless, not able to even change my own pants. Hell, I couldn't even scratch my own nose.

Cookie sat bolt upright in his wheelchair in a cast from his hips to his armpits that looked like a fibreglass suit of armour. It was decorated with all the young nurses' autographs, signed in Nikko pen. His arms and shoulders were ripped. He reminded me of Discobolus, the Greek discus-throwing statue, and I could understand why he was so popular with the young nurses.

But even as I lay there at his mercy, angry at the cigarette stunt he performed this and every morning, I still admired his strength. Not just his physical strength, but his attitude to life.

I knew I would never have his abs, pecs, or triceps, but there was no reason I couldn't have his attitude.

Sometimes I wished I were him, with his muscles, abilities, and independence.

"If only I were a para and not a quad." The thought made me envious of how much easier it would be if I could still use my hands.

Then I'd think about Bill.

"Well, at least I'm not Bill."

Truth is, we all had a massive hill to climb emotionally and physically before we would leave this place. It didn't really make that much difference emotionally whether you were a quad or a para.

Some of the biggest toughest blokes in the spinal unit cried themselves to sleep every night, while I never saw Bill without a smile on his face.

If we didn't make a miraculous recovery, each and every one of us would face our own individual Everest.

Then, one night, it happened.

"I can move my little finger," Andrew said excitedly.

"Bullshit," I said. "Show me."

He held his hand up in the air and wiggled his little finger.

"Bullshit!" I said again, but this time not in disbelief.

I was excited for Andrew, of course, but also excited by the prospect that the same might happen for me. He'd been here for a few weeks longer than me, so it was only right that he would get movement before I did.

Andrew continued to gain recovery. First his fingers, then his wrists. He started to gain muscles in his legs – he could even wiggle his toes!

I was even more excited at the prospect that this would be me very, very soon.

By the end of the first day, he could move all of his fingers, the day after that the fingers on his other hand; by the end of the week, he could move everything. The movement wasn't strong, but it was still movement. He had something to work with when he got out of bed and into the physio gym.

I waited for my turn for things to start to move.

All day and all night I waited. I had nothing else to do but wait and hope. Wait and hope I would catch up to my mate beside me.

During the days, the wait wasn't quite so bad; there was always something going on to distract me.

Doctors' rounds, medications, wound dressings, catheter changes, bed changes, bed baths, and turns. There were always the turns, every two or four hours.

Physiotherapists and occupational therapists would come around and stretch our limbs and fingers to keep our range of movement while we were still bed-bound.

Ah, but the nights. The long, lonely nights. The night waits were the worst.

Once the lights were turned off, there was nothing to distract me from my thoughts.

It's funny how some smells can take you back in time. In this place, there was one constant smell that didn't know the difference between night and day.

Forty-four people with no control of their bowels and doctors obsessed with relieving their constipation... The ward had a residual smell of faeces. In the dark and quiet of night, without your other senses to distract you, the stench of shit overwhelmed you.

The smell took me straight back to the late '60s, when the council dunny man would walk past my bedroom window in the early hours of the morning with a fresh clean shit tin full of sawdust. He'd walk back from the thunderbox in the back yard with the old one on his shoulder full of the week's deposits, a swarm of flies and that unforgettable odour following him up the driveway.

"I want to be a dunny man when I grow up," Jonny Mara would often say during morning tea at Richmond Hill State School. The dunny truck drove down Prior St about that time on its way out to the council depot. He thought they must get paid a lot of money to do that job.

I knew what I wanted to be, too. I was going to be a Park Ranger, just like Matt Hammond from Waratah National Park.

We hadn't even turned 10 years old, but already we were visualising our futures.

By the time I hit grade 6, I even knew who I was going to marry. Vikki Antaw. Well, I thought I did; her family moved away the next year and took with them my first true love.

By grade 12, I had a realistic and achievable vision of what my future was going to look like. It was very clear and detailed; I even knew most of the steps to make that dream a reality.

I would become a high school manual arts teacher; I'd never have to buy my own cigarettes again. I'd just confiscate them off the kids like my teachers did to me.

Lost Dreams

It was easy to become a manual arts teacher. All I had to do was do a trade – carpenter or plumber would be my preference – go to uni for a year, and that's it. Simple.

I'd meet the woman of my dreams at uni; we'd move back to Charters Towers and get a hobby farm on Sandy Creek. Johnny Mara would build my house with split-faced Besser blocks. He wouldn't get the opportunity to be the dunny man after the town finally got a sewerage system in 1975. I'd get my teaching job at State High, wear my polyester shorts, long socks, short-sleeve shirt and tie, and park the Honda XL250 under the big tamarind tree outside the woodwork room.

She'd be an accountant and work at the Commonwealth Bank. We'd have a couple of kids, a dog, veggie garden, the whole great Aussie dream. We'd have lots of friends and they'd have kids the same age.

I had it all worked out. I didn't want to be rich or famous, just a happily married family man with my little patch, a good job, and, of course, good health – that went without saying.

When I say "not rich" – I'd still be able to have a nice car, Holden Monaro of course, a Toyota Land Cruiser, and a boat. Maybe even a pool.

I would shoot clay targets at the gun club with my brand-new C grade Browning once a month.

Nowhere in the script did it say "become a quadriplegic." That wasn't part of the dream.

Just nine months after graduating high school, the first pieces were falling into place. I got a Drafting cadetship with the MRD in Cloncurry, not a "trade," but once I was a qualified draftsman, I could do the same course at uni to become a teacher. I didn't really care that much how I got there; I was on the way.

I'd met a girl in Mt Isa – not ideal being 100 km away, but still, it had potential.

I was well ahead of schedule; the rest would follow. I just knew it.

Then, in the blink of an eye, like some kind of macabre David Copperfield illusion, in a splash of Fletcher Creek water, it was all gone. Washed away forever.

With one tiny lapse of judgement, one slightly mistimed dive, my vision of the perfect future was erased. Permanently!

There could be no teaching job at Charters Towers State High School.

There could be no hobby farm on Sandy Creek, no veggie patch, no 4x4.

There could be no kids to wrestle on the front lawn.

How could I possibly have kids now? Who could ever love someone like this?

Everything was gone. I had no future!

I had nothing. Nothing but another god knows how many more weeks in head traction and more of those bloody turns.

Days and days of thinking about what could never be. Days and days of reliving that almost perfectly executed prank dive.

My nights were filled with dreams – or maybe they were thoughts, too. I couldn't tell the difference most of the time, and it didn't really matter. My head was just full of "what could have been" or "if only."

CHAPTER 3

BLOOD, SWEAT AND TEARS

Finally, the day arrived and my tongs were removed. It wasn't quite the euphoria I'd imagined.

Yes, the head traction was gone but, in its place, there was a hard-plastic neck collar that I had to wear for the next few weeks. I'm sure it was imbued with long-lasting, extra-strength itching powder just to prolong my torment.

"When can I get out of bed?" I asked Sue the physio, like the kid in the back seat of the car on a long trip demanding: "Are we there yet? Are we there yet?"

"You've got to build up the strength in your neck muscles for a few days, until you're able to hold your head off the pillow for a whole minute," Sue explained. "We'll start next week."

OH, FUCK. I'M SHIT AT THIS!

One of our drills at footy training was to lie on your back and hold your head and feet an inch off the ground.

I'm never going to get out of this stinking bed.

"Only a minute?" I said. "That sounds easy enough. Can I have a go now?" At least I could sound confident. "And then I can get up, right?"

"Yes, that's correct," she said. "I'll see you on Monday," she added, before turning to walk away.

"And you'll let me have a crack at it then?" I needed confirmation.

"We'll see," she said without stopping to turn around.

We'll see. She sounded just like Mum.

We'll see? We'll see alright.

I was determined to get up as soon as I possibly could.

There wasn't much sleep that night or the rest of the weekend. I had something to look forward to. I had a vision of the future again. Admittedly, it was nothing like my previous dream, but at least it was something to work on.

All I had to do was something I couldn't even do before I broke my neck. I tried lifting my head, and the pain forced me to lower it again immediately.

Eventually, Monday morning came around and I couldn't wait for Sue to arrive. I'd been practicing all weekend. Today would be the last time a nurse would dribble porridge down my face and scrape it up with the spoon in one motion, like a skilled mother feeding her child.

Today was the day I'd waited for, for almost three months.

"It's okay if you can't do it the first time." Sue was skilled at prepping her patients. "Most people take a few goes before they get it."

I'm not most people.

Something clicked in my brain, and I knew before I tried that a second attempt wouldn't be necessary.

I lifted my head off the pillow. Sue removed the collar and slipped her hand under my head.

"One-one thousand, two-one thousand, three-one thousand," she said, counting the seconds out loud.

I didn't hear her reach ten. I had fixed my gaze on a mouldy stain on the wall, turned off my pain sensors, and started my own count.

"…59-one thousand, 60-one thousand, 61-one thousand…" She stopped counting and said, "Okay, rest." She eased my head back down onto the pillow. "You did it first go." She seemed surprised. "That was very impressive. Let's get you up."

She called for the wardies to come and lift me out. The collar went back on and Bob lifted me into a sitting position. Sliding his arms under my armpits, he clasped my wrists. The other wardie got me under the knees. They "top and tail" lifted me into a wheelchair.

I was super excited to be in a wheelchair for the first time. Who would have thought that on that day, eleven short weeks ago, at footy training? It felt like years ago.

"Good morning, Colin." Cookie's voice was coming from this weird-looking bloke who resembled him a little bit. I'd only ever seen him through prism glasses from a lying down position.

Then I passed out.

Postural hypotension is common for people with spinal injuries when sitting up for the first few times.

I would regain consciousness with cold shower water running over my face most mornings for the next week or so.

Now the really hard work of rehabilitation would begin.

Now I would learn the real difference between paras and quads.

"Quads are useless," Cookie was always quick to remind me.

He was just like my father. The old man had a way of making me feel shit about myself whenever I stuffed up.

"What on earth possessed you to dive into the fucking Fletcher?"

It's the first thing Dad said to me after I had done just that and broken my neck. It's a question which had been haunting me ever since. It's a question I tried to answer for him in some logical way, but an answer never came. There was no logic to it.

Looking back, I now know how much of an impact my accident had on Dad. His only son was paralysed. His dreams for me were now gone, too, along with the prospect of a grandson to carry on the family name.

His son was a cripple! The "C" word was still commonly used. I'm still of the opinion that the Oxford Dictionary meaning (noun: Offensive. a term used to refer to a person who is partially or totally unable to use one or more limbs) is accurate, and I can't understand how it became politically incorrect.

A logical answer was never going to make up for Dad's loss, anyway, and I started to ask myself, "How can I make it up to him? How can I make my father proud of me?" I couldn't answer that, either.

Cookie had his own rhyming slang for cripple; he wasn't offended by it. "I'm a Choccy Ripple," he'd laugh and pucker his lips. "Sweet and tasty."

"Ha ha, that's funny. Me too." I wanted to be one of the boys.

"Sorry, you can't," he barked bluntly. "Quads aren't cool enough."

It was like an upstairs downstairs thing, where the paras thought that somehow they were better than the quads, just because they had more muscle function.

Maybe they were right. It was expected that most paraplegics, even though they might not regain any muscle recovery below their injury level, would be able to live independently and return to a functional, normal lifestyle after rehabilitation.

Most of us with neck injuries, the quads, didn't have so much to look forward to. There were some exceptions.

Andrew rapidly regained almost all of his muscle recovery, but he still experienced severe spasms and pain. He'd be able to live independently, but he would never be the same as he once was. He would still be cursed with the bladder and bowel issues we all live with. That kept us all on the same page.

Stud would be okay, but still not quite Choccy Ripple class. His injury level was just a little bit lower than mine. He had the use of his triceps. One muscle. It didn't seem much, but it meant the difference between independence or dependence. He would be able to live a normal life again. He proclaimed himself the "Super Quad" and could even get himself up off the floor without assistance if he fell. Not if, when. He fell out of his chair a lot.

Even after six months of intensive rehabilitation, my prospects were not good. Without triceps, there was no possibility I would ever live without someone to care for me.

Even though all the expert advice said otherwise, I made the decision I was going to prove them all wrong.

I was going to prove to Cookie that all quads aren't useless. I was going to become a Super Quad, too.

I was going to prove to the old man that I wasn't useless. I would find a way to make him proud of his son.

I was going to prove to all the therapists that you didn't need triceps to be independent.

"They're overrated. Triceps are for pussy paras." I called the paras out. "You wankers are only in it for the parking. Quads are the real deal, Choccy Ripples."

Now I had a challenge. Now I had to live up to my words. I had a glimpse of my old vision. I couldn't see it clearly, but I had to have a purpose in life. All I knew was, *I'm not going to let this stop me.*

Somehow my goal was never "to walk again." I guess at a subconscious level, I knew I wouldn't. But I would be the best C6 quad ever to not walk out of there.

Most weekdays I spent in the physio gym, building up the strength in the few muscles I had to work with. I had to learn how to sit up in bed and keep my balance without abdominal muscles. I had to learn how to transfer from my bed to my wheelchair. I had to learn how to dress myself.

At first, I struggled to even roll over by myself, but slowly, ever so slowly, I improved. Each day I grew stronger. Each day I stretched myself a little bit further.

If I wasn't in physio, I was in occupational therapy, or OT as it's generally called. OT was like some kind of sadistic torture chamber designed to frustrate you to the point of screaming.

There was lots of screaming.

How the hell can you teach someone to use their fingers to pick marbles out of a bowl of rice when their FUCKING FINGERS DON'T EVEN WORK?!

Annette, my OT, was on the receiving end of my frustration too many times, but she was just as determined as I was to help me reach my potential.

"Lift up your wrist and you'll see that your thumb will touch your first finger," she instructed. "It's called the Tenodesis grip. With practice you should be able to do a lot more than you think."

Sometimes I thought my hands were there purely for aesthetics, but I knew I had to learn how to make them function for me again.

The learning didn't stop with the therapists. Back on the ward, the nurses' role in my rehabilitation was just as important. I had to learn how to manage my bladder and bowels.

Thank God I'm not Gary, I thought with great relief. Gary was a para who left the physio gym early every single day to get cleaned up after a bowel accident. With lower level injuries like his, the back door was so much harder to keep closed than it was for the quads. Finally, something we could do better than them.

It was a different story altogether when it came to my bladder. With no hand function, I wouldn't be able to self-catheterise like they did. I had to use a "leg bag" attached – glued, actually – to my penis with a product called Skin Bond. If manscaping wasn't a thing back then, I was a pioneer. There was no place for pubic hair with that stuff.

There was so much to learn. All my everyday personal grooming and hygiene routine was a test that I had to figure out how to accomplish without functional fingers.

Rehabilitation was hard work both physically and mentally.

Fucking. Hard. Work.

But it wasn't all work and no play. Once the therapies were finished, of an afternoon one of us would usually call a taxi and send them down to the Norman Hotel to get a carton of

XXXX. There were a few weeks where we had to settle for some rather unsavoury brews during the famous beer strike of 1978, though.

We would set up a card game on the dining room table. The wardies would usually join us and play poker or blackjack, have a few beers, and smoke cigarettes. Nothing too rowdy.

"Can you open this for me, Cookie?" I hadn't mastered the Tenodesis grip enough to open my own beers.

"Open it yourself, you lazy little shit. I'm not always gunna be there to wipe your bum for you." Whether he knew it or not, Cookie was the best therapist I had, forcing me to problem solve and find a way.

What we were doing was putting the theory of our therapy sessions into our practical lives.

We were learning how to be normal again.

Dealing with the frustration of not being able to use my hands to hold the cards, or to light or even hold my own cigarette, became in itself a huge part of my challenge.

By the time August rolled around and my discharge date was in sight. Eleven long months of recovery and rehabilitation under my belt and I was still nowhere near independent.

Most of the tasks I needed to be able to perform, I still needed help with.

Yes, I could transfer in and out of bed, but not confidently on my own. Unlike Stud, I couldn't get up by myself if I fell.

Yes, I could dress my top half, but I still needed help with my pants, shoes, and socks.

I could eat my own dinner without losing my balance and falling face first into it. Up until that point, I had been a constant source of entertainment to everyone at meal times, often ending up with my nose planted into my dinner.

I could push my wheelchair across the road, just.

I could comb my hair and brush my teeth.

I could empty my own pee bag and manage my bowels, kind of.

There wasn't any more the therapists could help me with. It was time to go home.

Somewhere, another young bloke was breaking his neck to take my place here.

The rest I would have to do on my own.

Then came time for the discussion about where I would go after my discharge from hospital.

There were only two options.

I could go into a nursing home, like so many did. There were no funding schemes to support me to live independently. There was no NDIS in 1979.

I could move back in with Mum and Dad and have them care for me. This was obviously Mum's preferred option; she could fluff her feathers up and mother me again like a mother hen with her chickens.

Neither option sat well with me. I wanted my independence. I wanted to be like all my mates. None of them lived with their mums – but nevertheless, that's what I did. I moved home.

Mum and Dad had returned to Charters Towers several months before my discharge. They both had to go back to work.

They had been busy putting an extension on the house with a wheelchair-accessible shower and toilet. They built a ramp up the side so that I could get inside to the main living area, and they built a huge patio and outdoor living area. It was a real community effort. All our friends and family rallied around to get the job done.

There was no government assistance to help with home modifications, not that Dad would have taken it anyway.

That's what happened in small country towns – we looked out for each other.

The whole community must have thought I was such an ungrateful child when I told them the news that I had no intention of staying there.

I couldn't see myself living with my mum for the rest of my life. I'd left home already – as soon as I finished school, just like all my mates.

I wanted the dream again, or at least to be working towards it. One of the hardest things I found was not letting anyone help me. I knew then that if I let them help me, I would never learn to do it on my own.

Sorry, Mum, I can't be your chick.

My immediate mission in life was to be able to live without help, so I spent most of my time working out how I could independently do the things I needed to do to live on my own.

I just wanted to be normal.

During my rehabilitation at the spinal unit, I had the opportunity for a driving lesson in a car specially modified with hand controls. I'd always loved to drive. Actually, it was the first question I asked my doctors in the spinal unit.

Dr Vernon Hill, the assistant director of the spinal unit, was giving me "the talk."

"You have a fracture at the C6 level in your spine. It's early days yet, but there is a real possibility you may have sustained permanent damage to your spinal cord."

"Will I still be able to drive a car?" The thought of not being able to drive was my most pressing concern.

"Ho ho ho." He had a jolly Santa Claus laugh. "I thought you'd want to know if you could still get an erection!" Apparently, that was the question most of the young blokes asked.

"Oh yeah, that too." Then I figured if I had a flash car, the other wouldn't matter so much.

Dr Hill had a special interest in sex and fertility after spinal cord injury, not that I thought I would ever be a suitable candidate for his work.

"Yes, you should be able to," he answered, adding in his Professor Julius Sumner Miller style, "I know a few patients with your injury level who drive. You may not be able to get your wheelchair in on your own, though."

Mum always parked her old EH wagon under the mango tree in the back yard. It was only about 9:00 in the morning, but already the mercury was pushing 90 degrees Fahrenheit on the old thermometer hanging from one of its branches.

I gave myself instructions. "Today's task is to get yourself in the car, fold up your wheelchair and put it in the car, then take it out again and get out. And repeat."

I studied the car seat and remembered how easily I had climbed over the seat the night I lost my virginity at the Tors Drive-In. Ah, she had some memories, the old girl, but now was not the time for nostalgia. I was on a mission.

A one-day job turned into two and then three before I finally mastered it. I'd have to figure it out all over again when I got my own car. Mum's EH was manual. I would need an auto.

Three days of blood, sweat – lots of sweat – and tears. Three days of frustration but determination. I had to do this.

The neighbours must have thought "like father, like son." Dad used to park the cars in the same spot to do regular services and maintenance on them.

We both had the same arsenal of profanities to deal with our frustration. We both had the same short fuse before we exploded, but we also both had the same determination to finish the job.

My chance to leave home came a lot earlier than I expected.

Before leaving the spinal unit, my social worker had submitted an application on my behalf to the Taringa Rehabilitation centre. I got accepted, which meant I could move back to Brisbane before I was fully independent.

I jumped at the opportunity. I could dot the i's and cross the t's there.

Mum cried just as much as she did at the Charters Towers railway station, the day I left home the first time…

Maybe a little more.

CHAPTER 4
ONE OF THE BOYS

Cookie, Fossil, Slug, Froggie, Tommy Triangle... Even "Shagger" was there (Stud had changed his name to Shagger, which better suited his physical attraction than his prowess with the ladies). Most of the boys from the old spinal wards S7 and S8 at the PA were there, along with about 70 other "clients" with a variety of disabilities, not just spinal.

Taringa Rehab was a lot different to the spinal unit rehab. The focus was very much targeted at occupational outcomes rather than just physical recovery and activities of daily living, or ADLs, as they liked to call them.

Neither place paid much attention to the emotional or psychological rehabilitation which was so desperately needed. I doubt our egos would have embraced it, anyway. Us blokey blokes knew that the best way to get our emotions in check was to get busy and not think about it.

I knew in my head what I needed to do here. I had no time to get upset and start feeling sorry for myself. I was here to tick three boxes to successfully complete my rehabilitation and get my life back on track.

Employment. Accommodation. Transport.

Tick. Tick. Tick. And I'd be good to go.

I started to see a future for myself slowly emerging out of the shattered wreckage of my high school vision.

I hadn't given much thought to returning back to work until now. The MRD had put me on a superannuation pension. I was receiving 75 percent of my wage and that would continue until I turned 65 if I chose. Forty-five years on the pension – that wasn't part of my dream. Luckily for me, and my vision, I did have the option of returning to work if I wanted to. I wanted to.

Employment: tick!

Now all I had to do was figure out how I was going to get there and where I was going to live.

In 1980, Brisbane's public transport system was not wheelchair accessible at all. No buses, no trains, not even a Maxi Taxi. I would need my own car.

Cookie found an early model GTS Monaro, bright yellow with black racing stripes, in the Trading Post and made his own hand controls with a couple of sticks and a piece of heavy fishing line. Fossil got an advance on his CTP payout and bought a V12 XJS Jag. Their priorities were more about attracting members of the opposite sex than going back to work.

I had been saving up my pension to buy my first ever car. I had a little over $5,000 in the bank. Like Cookie, I found a '76 V8 Monaro in the Trading Post which was within my budget.

Yes. A V8 Monaro was part of my original plan. I had no way of getting out to have a look at it. I certainly wasn't going to pay for a taxi all the way to Springwood and back, so my physio said he'd go take a look at it for me.

"Nice car, but it's got no power steering," he said. "You won't have the strength to turn the steering wheel. Not without triceps."

So that plan was crushed.

Common sense prevailed – or maybe it was more that Dad said, "You need something reliable so you won't break down. Get a new 4 cylinder."

I started to become aware that my new vision might have to look a bit different to the original. I could always trade up when I got the strength.

The shiny new white 1980 Honda Civic was delivered to the front reception at the rehab centre. She was a sight to behold: $5,095 on the road, fitted with custom built "push-pat" hand controls. I had only ever smelt that "new car" smell once before, when Dad bought the '74 Toyota Land Cruiser and drove it down the driveway that first time. Oh, I hoped she would have some stories to tell over the next ten years, this little car.

The thing I loved most about driving was that once I was in the car, I was no longer "the wheelchair guy" unless you knew me. There was no way of telling that I was in any way different to any of the other drivers on the road. Driving gave me that sense of being normal, even to the point where sometimes after a long trip, I'd open the door and try to get out of the car, forgetting I needed my wheelchair.

It's a bit like trying to get out without taking off the seatbelt. *Oh shit, that's right, ha ha ha.*

Transport: tick! Two down, one to go.

Finding somewhere to live was going to be the biggest hurdle. I had heard of a house in Hamilton, "Wheelie 1," purpose built for people with a spinal injury who weren't quite independent. Bill was already living there. That would have been the perfect halfway house for me until I got the skills and confidence to do it alone. I applied for a place, but there was a waiting list as long as your arm – not surprising, really, since it was the only one in the state.

Every Saturday morning, Cookie, Gordon and I would get the *Courier-Mail*, make ourselves a cup of coffee, and scroll through the rental properties.

"There's a share house called 'Montarosa' at Highgate Hill – paraplegic wanted, it says." Gordon had found the perfect place. We all applied and went to a group interview.

"You haven't got any triceps, have you?" It wasn't a question. It was a rejection. "You won't be able to live here."

Gordon moved in the next day.

Cookie and I went back to the classifieds until, one day, he found a two-bedroom flat in West End.

"It's got a few stairs and the bathroom needs some work, but I can fix that up." He winked and flexed his biceps. "I can't afford 60 bucks a week, though; you're gunna have to come share the rent with me."

"So, you are going to be around to wipe my bum for me, then." I felt smug throwing his words back at him.

"Don't be a smartarse or I'll tip you out of your chair." He was serious.

Gordon borrowed some tools from his brother and helped Cookie build a ramp to the front door of this flat and the one next door. As it turned out, the flat next door became vacant during the ramp construction; Gordon left Montarosa and became our neighbour. Once I got inside the flat, I saw that the bathroom wasn't that bad and I could manage with only a little bit of hassle. Cookie got a sledge hammer and took out the brick wall anyway. He liked to do things that involved physical strength. This wouldn't be the last time we would "make over" a rental property.

Accommodation: tick!

While I had ticked off employment from my list, I still hadn't actually been into the office at this point.

The big day arrived. I wasn't quite ready. Our flat didn't have a laundry, so I had to buy some new "work" clothes; I'd been wearing the same jeans for about a week now. We hadn't set up the kitchen, so we were still living on takeaways. I'm not sure whether I had "butterflies" in the tummy from the nerves, dodgy reheated takeaways, or my new pants were a size too small – I just felt a bit off that day.

I parked the car over the freshly painted white wheelchair symbol on my allocated parking spot on the basement level of the MRD building in Spring Hill. Only top-level public servants had their own parking space. They were signposted with their job title.

"Mine's got my picture on it," I chuckled to myself sarcastically. "I must be the most important one here."

Taking extra care not to get my clothes dirty, I slid my wheelchair across my lap and onto the ground beside me, and transferred out of the car. I looked up to the seventh floor, where I was about to meet my new work colleagues for the first time, and took a moment to feel good about how far I'd come. Then, for the briefest of seconds, I heard Mum saying, "Don't get too cocky. You don't want to fall," and the thought was gone.

Monday, 22 September 1980, almost two years to the day I broke my neck. And here I was, back to where I'd left my dream. Well, there was that minor detail involving a girl but I still had no real interest in a relationship, even though I'd fallen in and out of love with one of my therapists and half the student nurses at the spinal unit during my time in traction.

Geoff Smethurst, second in charge of the drafting department, met me at the lift and took me around the room to introduce me to the team.

"Brian, Col. Col, Brian."

"G'day, Brian," I said, in my blokiest voice, as I extended my hand, trying my hardest to get my limp fingers into his hand far enough before he squeezed them and looked up with that look. You know, the one blokes give when they receive a soft handshake and make that initial judgement about your sexuality.

"Alex, Col."

"Geoff, Phil, Rod..." There were about a dozen draftees working in this section.

I was trying to make my best first impression and remember 12 new names, which wasn't my forte, when that unmistakable smell rose up. Being a good foot shorter than everyone else, I got it first. I could feel my face going white as the blood drained out and then bright red as the embarrassment of this public humiliation took over like a cuttlefish flashing its warning to a predator.

"It's really nice to meet you all, but I'll be off home now," I managed to say, as I turned and pushed as fast as I could towards the lift, hoping – no, praying – that the source of the smell wasn't running down the leg of my pants and onto the floor. I didn't look back to see. No one tried to follow me, and I can't say I blamed them.

I'd shit my pants, but that wasn't the worst of it. I had no way of cleaning myself up here, so I had to get in the car to go home. There goes that new car smell. Once home, I had to get into bed to get undressed – the sheets needed changing anyway – and into the shower to wash the remaining shit off myself.

The rest of that day was spent washing and drying my clothes, my sheets, my car seat covers. Luckily for me, the laundromat on Gladstone Road had great parking and easy access.

"That's one way to make a good impression, Colin." Cookie was pissing himself laughing.

On Tuesday, I invented Groundhog Day, 13 years before the movie. I did exactly the same thing as the day before. Everyone was way too polite to say anything or ask what had happened. They didn't get the chance; I shit myself again and left in a hurry, just as I had on day one. Back in the car, back into bed, back into the shower. Wash clothes, wash sheets, wash seat covers, tell Cookie to "Shut the fuck up. It's not funny."

I never knew anyone could be so full of shit, literally. The same thing happened on the Wednesday. I started to know how Gary felt. Even Cookie didn't laugh this time.

I was totally exhausted by hump day of my first week back at work, but somehow, I got through to the weekend. I remember that horror week as if it were yesterday, but that's not how my old MRD colleagues remembered me.

"How many times did you fall out of your wheelchair on the weekend, Yobbo?" Beetle asked every Monday morning. Well, the Mondays I showed up at least.

I was one of the team. I had a nickname. Yobbo. Everyone had a nickname, but not all names were used to their face. There was an "us and them" here, too, but this time I was one of the cool kids.

We had "Rocket" Rod, "Beetle," "the Flea," and Al "Forna" Caton, while the bosses and career boys had "G1" and "G2," the two Geoffs; "Shed," short for Shithead; and "Quit," short for fuckwit.

I slotted right into the "public servant" stereotype. Flexitime suited my lifestyle like a glove, although I "flexed off" a lot more Friday afternoons than I ever worked up credit for. No one ever pulled me up on it; maybe it was a pity thing. I didn't care. I milked it to the limits.

The International Hotel was only a couple of doors up Boundary Street from the office, and every Friday lunch hour they had topless girls selling raffle tickets. Every Friday most of the team took a two-hour lunch to support the cause. Every Friday, I stayed after they went back to work. I wasn't trying to hit on the girls; I still didn't see myself as boyfriend material, and I don't think most of them saw me in that way, either. It was kind of fun to look at their titties, though. I did have a connection with Billie, and she would often stay and have a few beers with me after she put her clothes back on. Our connection never got close enough for her to tell me her real name, though.

The police crackdown on drink driving hadn't come into effect then, so I usually drove from there to meet the boys after work at one of our regular hangouts in the city. Then I'd hit a nightclub or the Brisbane City Council Club until late, and in the early hours of the next morning I'd drive home, of course.

Some of my old high school mates had moved to Brisbane, too, and Saturday nights we'd look for pubs that were more like the ones back home. The Sunnybank Tavern or the Glen Hotel. Sundays we'd do the pub sessions at places like Victoria Point, Broadbeach, or Bribie Island, drink beer, and play pool. I was normal, just like all my mates. Working five days a week and on the piss all weekend.

We drank mostly because that's what young blokes our age did. But I also drank to compensate for the realisation that I didn't have the dexterity in my fingers and hands to complete my drafting cadetship. I was reassigned from engineering to the clerical department.

As much as I didn't want to believe it, I wouldn't ever become a high school teacher, not the way I thought I would, anyway. That part of the picture was rapidly fading back into the mist. True, I had a job for life at the MRD – but not as a draftsman.

Part of the program at the Taringa Rehab Centre involved sporting activities, and it was there that I met Roy "Chook" Fowler, a much more travelled man than my old footy mate of the same name. Chook was the Australian Wheelchair Archery champion and represented his country in several other events in track and field. He introduced me to the sport of "club throwing," an event restricted to quadriplegics only.

Wheelchair athletes were classified into different classes based on their muscle function and balance. There was even a class just for people with little or no use of their triceps. I was seriously interested now. Chook taught me all he knew about throwing the club. We would never compete against each other; he was classed as the next level up. My competitive nature kicked in, and I got the desire to push hard and see how far I could get in this new, tailor-made sport.

Somehow, in among working full time, socialising at least three days a week, and keeping up with my domestic duties, I found time to train. Two nights every week, I trained in the Sporting Wheelies gym in West End. Two afternoons a week after work, I practiced my throwing technique at the warm-up track of the still under-construction QEII stadium.

Cookie and Gordon weren't interested in athletics. To tell the truth, they both smoked way too much pot to have a serious focus on much of anything. They were quite content to stay at home and pull cones most days. I didn't mind the odd joint or two, but not enough to want to do it all day.

Shagger, on the other hand, was a natural athlete and took to the track like a duck to water. He even had his own purpose-built track chair. Shagger lived on his own in a two-bedroom flat in Taringa, just down the hill from the rehab centre, and worked full time at the Wesley hospital. It didn't take much convincing for him to let me move in with him, and we became the two super quads training and living together.

Some nights I trained so hard I barely had the strength left to get myself into the car. Driving home using the hand controls was really quite dangerous. My arms were often so weak I couldn't push the brakes. "Fuck, I hope you stay green," I'd say to every traffic light on the way home, or shout out loud, "Go green, go green!" if the light was red. Either way, I rarely stopped.

In our first year, we both got selected in the Queensland team to compete in the national titles in Melbourne. I was thrilled. This was the first time I'd left the state, other than to drive to Tweed just to cross the border. The Melbourne trip was a real eye opener. The Queensland team had tremendous team spirit coming off the back of the inaugural rugby league State of Origin and took out the blue-ribbon event, wheelchair basketball, against the home state in an upset. Shagger won a silver medal in the 200-meter track and gained selection in the national relay team to compete in Hong Kong.

In my event, the 1A Club Throw, the competition was world class. Wayne Patchett, the NSW representative, was the reigning world record holder and easily won the event. I won the silver medal and a bronze in the discus – not enough to gain selection in the Australian team, though. I was named as a shadow player, which was a bit like being the twelfth man in the cricket team. You're in the team, but you don't get to play or travel away unless someone pulls out.

Not long after the team was announced, Patchett withdrew due to work commitments. Yes! I was in. Now I'd have to find more time in my hectic schedule to fit in a few extra training sessions. Shagger and I trained together after work wherever we could. New Farm Park was a great place to go for a push and a throw; we even used the car park at Buranda shopping centre on a Sunday when it wasn't busy.

The Qantas Jumbo was almost full, with over 200 athletes and staff in the biggest Australian team ever. I felt like Mick Dundee, the crocodile man, as we dropped into Hong Kong after a nine-and-a-half-hour flight. It seemed like we were landing in the middle of Salisbury Road. "Faaaark!" I couldn't help the Graham Kennedy crow call as we flew in past the tallest buildings I had ever seen.

After falling out of my chair during the opening ceremony, the competition for me was a bit of a non-event. There were no other competitors from other countries in any of my events. I got to join Shagger in the 200 relay and race against ourselves. I felt cheated that I didn't get to beat anyone. I was embarrassed that I'd won four gold medals for my country in front of the Duke and Duchess of Kent. I felt unworthy of being a gold medallist and didn't wear my medals on the way home like the other athletes. I didn't compete again after that.

Somehow, after all I'd achieved over the last two years – relearning how to take care of myself, returning to full time work, getting my first car, and being accepted as an equal with my mates and work colleagues – I still felt inadequate. It was this disappointment which had the greatest impact on my self-esteem.

Just like most newspapers, my front-page story was a negative one. You needed to search deep to find a feel-good story.

Yesterday Today Tomorrow

CHAPTER 5
THE GREAT AUSSIE DREAM

For the last four years since my injury, I'd been fighting a physical battle to recreate my old life and fulfil my old dreams. I still hadn't fully come to the realisation that I never would, certainly not in the same way I had pictured it.

I would have to compromise – no, reframe – those old pictures to be able to achieve them.

I'd already unwittingly been doing it. I had a Honda Civic, not a Monaro. I was a purchasing clerk, not a draftsman. I lived in a flat in Brisbane, not a farm on Sandy Creek.

I had already proven to myself and everyone else that I was physically capable of living an independent, successful life, even without the use of triceps or all the other undesired traits which came with my disability.

My desire to lead a normal, if not reframed, life was as strong as it had ever been, but always in the back of my mind. Competing with that desire was my low self-esteem and the feeling of being unworthy of the life I wanted.

Even as a child, I wasn't encouraged to feel good about myself or worthy of great things. We couldn't afford much new stuff, so we made do with what we had. That's just how it was in those days. That upbringing taught me to value the things I did have, but it also established a lower level of self-worth. I was encouraged to set humble goals within reach of our means, not to reach for the stars and be disappointed when I didn't get there.

Prior to my injury I was healthy, fit, and good looking, but even so, I wasn't that confident when it came to girls. I would rather not ask for a date than ask and be rejected. It's no surprise, now I was in a wheelchair, that I thought of myself as even less attractive to the opposite sex. The first thing I did after my accident was break up with my girlfriend. She could easily find someone more worthy than me.

I didn't feel worthy of an intimate relationship. Hell, I'd already dragged my baby sister, my mum and dad, and my family into a life they hadn't chosen.

There was always this underlying feeling of worthlessness.

Not pity. I never pitied myself.

I just couldn't love the physical person I'd become.

I couldn't love this body.

Where I once had a six-pack now looked more like a keg. With no abdominal muscles, I couldn't suck it in even if I tried. It was the same for most quadriplegics. There was even a name for it. "Quad Pod."

I couldn't see how anyone, other than my mother, could love this.

Even with such a low opinion of myself, somehow, I still pictured a wife in my dream. Maybe there was someone out there with equally low expectations.

In the same four-year period, Cookie and Gordon had lots of girlfriends.

"A wheelchair is a better chick magnet than a puppy," Cookie boasted proudly. He'd had a string of girlfriends and was very sexually active. I never had "the game" Cookie had, but he did help me to put myself out there, even if I still wasn't convinced I had anything to offer in a relationship.

It didn't take me long to find out that Cookie was right. There were a lot of girls out there who could see past the wheelchair. There were a lot who couldn't, though.

Cookie's theory went even further. He said, "There's heaps of chicks out there who want to tick 'fuck a wheelchair guy' off their bucket list." That was true too.

My abilities as a lover could be summed up in one word: clumsy. It's hard to be spontaneous when you have the added complication of a leg bag glued to your penis.

Nothing is insurmountable, though, and with a little forward planning I found it wasn't such a big issue, at least physically. I still had a serious mental hang-up over it.

Making love for me looked nothing like it does in the movies. Even if I'd had a signature move before, I couldn't have made those same moves after. I certainly couldn't do the one-handed, behind the back bra release. My repertoire was limited to a couple of basic positions – basic, but effective.

The one thing I had in my favour that even "Casanova" Cookie didn't was that I could still get an erection without needing to use pills or injections. That discovery came not long after Dr Hill had raised it – not literally – with me back in the spinal unit.

Sister Helen Morrow was the main urology nurse responsible for catheter changes and care. Thinking back, there was rarely a time when she hadn't stimulated an erection and grasped it firmly for much longer than necessary.

Yes, there definitely were women who had a sexual thing for boys with spinal injuries.

For months, I put Cookie's theories through rigorous testing. I enjoyed numerous short, and shorter, term relationships. I came up with a theory of my own that I call the Law of Unattraction. I found that most times I really put in the effort – dressed up, shaved, a splash of Brut 33, used my best polite pickup lines – by the end of the night, I went home alone.

On the other hand, those nights I didn't really give a shit about picking up, the nights I ended up quite pissed and just a tiny bit obnoxious, I usually got lucky. I never understood why "good girls" were attracted to "bad boys."

On those nights, we didn't always go back to my place. Sometimes I would go back to hers. One time I had to bum my way up a flight of stairs to the bedroom. By the time I got there, I was too tired to do anything more. I still had work to do on my stamina.

Then, one night at the Brisbane City Council Club, it happened. I met a beautiful French girl, Monique. We hit it off and started to see a lot of each other. She saw "me," not my wheelchair. Most nights I would drive out to Mitchelton and park outside her mum's house, and we'd sit in the car and talk for hours. I never got used to her mum's Doberman, who would silently appear beside the window and Woof! at me every time.

Monique's family was small, just her mum and two sisters. She was the baby. They all approved of her choice in me as her boyfriend, although I'm not convinced her mum ever really did. We spent the most time with her closest sister and her husband; in fact, it was her sister who did the matchmaking to get us together.

After only a few months, we started talking about getting married. *I'd better introduce you to Mum and Dad and the family I suppose.* A quick road trip to Charters Towers followed. Needless to say, Monique was a hit with my family. The whole town embraced her. We made the front page of the *Northern Miner*, the local newspaper, with a headline that read "From Pain to Pleasure." How they came up with that, I'll never know.

Not long after, my family and some of their friends flew to Brisbane for our wedding. Gordon scrubbed up alright to be my best man and the Jag looked even better as the wedding car.

We couldn't afford a honeymoon and moved straight into a flat in Fairfield. Married life was good. Like most young couples, our dream was to own our own home, so we scraped up enough for a deposit on a home loan and built a house in Alexandra Hills. All of our savings were put into the house. We barely had enough left for an Amart bed and a dining room table. We couldn't even afford curtains or floor coverings. They would have to come later, as we transformed our house into a home.

Both of us worked in public service and commuted to the city each day, just like hundreds of other young couples living in the outer suburbs of Brisbane. We were a two-income family. On the weekends, we had a busy social life with lots of "DINK" friends, and there always seemed to be a family gathering to go to.

Almost without realising what had happened, I had dropped into the "Great Aussie Dream."

Nine to five job, with an annual holiday to the Sunshine Coast.

Our own home in the suburbs, complete with Hills hoist and BBQ. (We didn't have the picket fence.)

No dog yet, but it would come once we had a fence. (It wasn't going to be a Doberman, that was for sure.)

Wife and 2.3 children. Oops. Hold the bus.

It wasn't long before the "C" word came up in discussion. I was sure we'd already talked about this. Our relationship took a serious hit once it was clear that Monique wanted a family and I wasn't able to be a father.

Not even a year after our wedding, we were separated and soon to be divorced on the grounds of irreconcilable differences. It was a lot more complicated than just that one thing, but in the end, I think we were just two young kids who didn't really know what they wanted. We realised we didn't want each other and did something about it.

Whenever anyone asked why we broke up, I told them "I was too tight to buy an anniversary present."

The split was very amicable. There wasn't much to settle apart from the house and the mortgage. Gordon had finally received his CTP payout and offered to take over Monique's half.

I spent some time reflecting on that year and started to ask myself some serious questions before going on to answer them.

Am I not husband material? No, not if you can't be a father. To me, the two words meant the same thing.

What made me believe that I couldn't be a father? I could get an erection but not ejaculate, but did that really mean there was no way I could be a father? No one had ever had the fertility conversation with me in the spinal unit. Dr Vernon Hill had tried on several occasions to bring up the topic, but at the time I wasn't even thinking I could ever have a girlfriend, let alone children.

I wonder if it's too late. I wonder if all my sperm are dead now? I had to find out for sure. I made an appointment to see Dr Hill.

My teenage concept of how to make a baby was so far away from this process you could be forgiven for thinking there was no similarity at all. Sure, I'd masturbated before; I was an expert at it from about 15 years of age up until my injury. I hadn't really given it a red-hot crack since; without a decent grip in my hands, I was never going to give myself a happy ending.

Dr Hill's procedure room was very clinical, not at all like the little rooms at the fertility clinic with the girlie magazines and KY gel.

"You know I'm not going to get any sexual pleasure out of this," Vernon said as he picked up a vibrator, which looked more like the grinder in my tool box.

"I'm sure I'm not either," I replied without taking my stare off the weapon in his gloved hand, *What the fuck's he going to do with that?*

Until now, I hadn't considered that this would be the first time I'd have sex with a man. Sure, Cookie and I had kissed with tongues before, but this time I was stone cold sober.

Brrrrrrrrrrrrrrrrrrrrrrrrrrrrrrrrrrrr! The vibrator started.

Vernon gave me a running commentary of the technique. We were on first name terms now; it would be too kinky calling him Dr Hill. "Let me know if you get too uncomfortable and I'll stop."

Not much seemed to be happening for some time, but he assured me he had a few more tricks up his sleeve. I started to feel a knot low in my tummy and it slowly grew in intensity. I tried not to moan. As this feeling intensified, I could feel my blood pressure rising in my head – both heads. My legs straightened with spasm and a faint headache made me let out a soft moan. The pressure built up rapidly, and before I knew it, my head was banging, my face was contorted with the pain, and my moans got louder. Just when I was about to "tap out," my toes curled up, the knot in my tummy wrenched tight with a force that brought my moan to an "ARRGH!," and my knees jumped up, almost knocking Vernon out.

I just described the "cum shot" scene from every porno film ever made.

"We'd better check your blood pressure." It was 220 something. "Let's sit you up and give you something for that. That's your autonomic dysreflexia, it should pass in a minute or two." My BP dropped back to normal quickly.

There was still just this one minor detail, though; there was no semen. I didn't ejaculate.

"I think we might have had success," Vernon said enthusiastically. "You've probably had a retrograde ejaculation. It's quite common. Let's have a look what's in your bladder." He inserted a catheter and drained the contents of my bladder. "I'll take a look under the microscope; I won't be long."

"Have I got time for a smoke?" I asked him with a wink.

The look on Vernon's face, when he returned, was one I'll never forget. He had a huge grin from ear to ear, and his genuine excitement flowed into his voice, "You've got swimmers!"

Well, now I knew. What a shame I didn't have a wife.

I was physically and mentally drained.

I drove home to tell Gordon the good news.

"You need a cone to celebrate!"

He never needed an excuse.

CHAPTER 6
SEX, DRUGS, AND ROCK 'N' ROLL

With Gordon's newfound wealth from his CTP payout, there was never a shortage of pot in the house. There was always a full mull bowl, Tally-Hos, and bong on the kitchen bench or dining room table.

The stench of bong water filled every room. It was like he'd used it in the mop bucket over the bare concrete floor. Monique and I never got to put down any carpet or tiles, and maybe it was just as well. We would never have been able to remove the stench.

We didn't need a lot of furniture. Well, I didn't. Gordon liked to get out of his chair as much as he could, so he bought a new leather lounge suite and as big a TV and sound system as would fit in the room. He fancied himself as a bit of a guitar player, so a Fender Stratocaster and amp found their way into the room beside the lounge.

Gordon bore an uncanny resemblance to Jimi Hendrix, but unfortunately for my ears, and the neighbourhood's, that's where the similarities ended. I would often drive home from work and hear a screeching version of "All Along the Watchtower" from two blocks away.

I need a cone, I'd tell myself, not because I've had a tough day at the office but because I needed it to cope with the noise he was making. By 7 o'clock most nights, we were both wasted and rummaging through the kitchen cupboards looking for something to cure the munchies.

There was never much there. Luckily for us, there was a Chinese takeaway at Capalaba which delivered, and most nights that's what we ate. Gordon usually ordered extra so that there would be something there for the next time we searched, but somehow it vanished before dinner time rolled around again.

Our evening meal was always washed down with a shot of expensive whiskey or cognac and at least one more cone. God knows how I got myself into bed each night, but I rarely fell onto the floor. When I did, that's where I stayed until morning, when Gordon would somehow manage to help me get back in my chair.

Gordon liked a breakfast cereal he'd had when he was a kid living in South Africa, called semolina. I'd never heard of it. We only ever had Uncle Toby's with butter and golden syrup.

Most mornings he would get up reasonably early and cook enough for the both of us. I doubt he was cooking it the way it was meant to be, because it tasted to me like the disgusting bland powder Mum used to mix up for my little sister when she was a baby.

By the time I finished my morning routine of showering, toileting, and dressing, I never usually had too much time for breakfast. I'd grab a quick coffee, and Gordon always insisted that I have a cone with him before I left for the day.

Without a clear vision for my own future any more, I found I easily slipped into being a part of Gordon's.

While I was at work during the day, a constant stream of visitors came to the house. Gordon had become the local dealer, buying his marijuana in pound bags and breaking it up into one ounce "deals." Unbeknown to me, he was buying and selling a lot more than just pot. He had access to any substance he liked.

I never really liked pot that much, although I never refused it when it was offered. My main issue was its inconsistency. Sometimes you'd have to smoke half a bag to get high and other times one cone would render me useless for hours. I would much rather go to the pub all day and know exactly how much it took for me to get pissed. Not much, really; I was a bit of a lightweight when it came to alcohol. Even though I knew my limit, I rarely stopped at it.

With all the booze and pot I was using, my personal grooming and dress code took a real dive. After my initial head shave in hospital to accommodate the skull tongs, I had only ever had my hair trimmed, and now I wasn't even doing that. My long, greasy locks hung in thick ringlets down past my shoulders. Instead of combing or brushing, I wore a headband, just like you would have seen on a '70s hippy love child. It was roughly made from an old Jackie Howe singlet.

Smoking pot eased my spasms but exaggerated the neuropathic pain in my feet, so I stopped wearing shoes. The upper legs on my jeans were worn through, but new clothes weren't high on the shopping list.

I wore the same clothes to work that I wore to the pubs or clubs. Ripped Levi 501s, a T-shirt or singlet, a headband, and no shoes. I had a special plaited leather "going out" headband.

Most days I only went to work to get over my hangover. My latest job at the MRD was an administrative assistant in the map room, but there wasn't much for me to do. Mostly I slept at my desk, way back in the darkest, quietest corner. No one in the private sector would've put up with that kind of work ethic. Getting fired from the public service was like getting dropped from the Australian cricket team; it was easier to get in then it was to get out.

My life now revolved mostly around pubs and clubs, and I tried not to spend much time at home with Gordon and his druggy mates.

I spent a lot of nights sleeping in the car and going to work in the same clothes as I wore out that night. My pillow and blanket lived permanently in the car, and I was able to drop the seat back far enough to be able to sleep comfortably through the night. Most times I was too drunk to know the difference anyway.

Everywhere I went, people wanted to buy me drinks. I always felt like it was because I was in a wheelchair and therefore out of pity, so at first I never accepted the charity. After a while, I decided, *Hey, if you're stupid enough to buy me a drink because I'm in a wheelchair, then I'm stupid enough to take it from you.* My MRD pay packet would never have kept up with this lifestyle anyway.

I wasn't aware of it at the time, but my new lifestyle had consumed my childhood dream and was now starting to nibble away at my independence. An independence I fought for so fearlessly only a couple of short years before.

Some of the young girls I worked with were into ska music. I'd never heard of ska but would have blindly followed them to a Backstreet Boys concert. One night they took me to Easts Leagues Club to a Strange Tenants concert. They were arguably the best home-grown Aussie ska band.

I fell in love with them – well, in love with their music and the "rude boys" look. Ska was the mother to rocksteady and reggae in the 1950s. My hippy look didn't fit in at all with the Bluebeat scene, so the hair had to come off. I went from shoulder-length ringlets to a number two blade all over.

The only other thing I needed to change was to get a pair of Doc Martens on my feet. Doc Martens were way out of my budget, and I wouldn't have been able to put them on myself anyway, so I remained shoeless.

Easts was the home of ska in Brisbane, and I found myself there three or four nights a week. It was also the home of the Tigers rugby league team. Not my old Cloncurry Tigers, but they wore the same jersey. Some weekends I would watch a home game and then spend the night inside the club skanking to a ska band, dancing, drinking rum, smoking weed, and trying to pick up. Rude boys dance rough. I usually fell out, or got knocked out of, my chair four or five times a night.

It was one of those nights I had my first real run in with the law. I'd been pulled over for speeding a few times but this time it was a little bit more serious.

I had created a self-test to ensure I was sober enough to drive. It was simple, if I could manage to unlock the door and get myself in and put my wheelchair in, I was sober enough to drive. Easier said than done, even when I was sober. This night I didn't pass the test and had fallen onto the ground in the process. I was as drunk as I'd ever been in my life.

"What do you think you're doing down there?" The copper's voice sobered me up enough to answer him.

"Tryna get inda bed," I slurred. He looked into the car and saw my pillow and blanket.

"So, you're not planning on driving your car, then?" He asked.

"Course not. I'm too pissed ta get in the fucker, how do ya think I'd be able to drive it?"

His partner got out of the car and the two of them picked me up and put me into my car.

"Can you throw me chair in too? Someone might steal it."

"Don't even think about trying to drive until morning," he ordered.

"Goodnight, officers."

As soon as they drove away, I started the car and went to drive out of the car park. The cops were waiting around the corner. The blue light and siren came on and they pulled me over. After returning to the station and undergoing the official breathalyser test, I spent the night in the Herschel Street watch house. It was surprisingly wheelchair accessible.

The next morning, I had to front the Magistrates Court, unwashed, unshaven, and wearing the same clothes I'd slept in. My favourite "International Marijuana Growers Association" T-shirt, not the most appropriate attire to wear facing a mid-range drink driving charge.

A $300 fine and one-month suspension. The magistrate was lenient as it was my first ever court appearance.

Gordon drove me to work for the next month, which meant I was spending the evenings at home with him or only going out to places that he wanted to go to. Rock concerts were his thing, and most weekends we would go to a concert or see a band playing at one of the suburban pubs.

There was none better than the Noosa Aussie Hop, which featured Midnight Oil, Mental as Anything, Skyhooks, the Church, Choir Boys, and others. That was one concert to remember, but it was also the first time I tried gold top mushrooms.

We'd travelled up to the concert the night before and stayed at a friend's place in Noosa. Someone made us a cup of coffee which tasted like it had dirt in it. The taste was stewed up magic mushrooms. I can't explain the way it made me feel. Certainly nothing like getting high on weed. I couldn't sleep.

I wandered around the streets in the drizzling rain all night and returned just in time to leave for the concert. It seemed like it was impossible to run out of energy.

I'll do this again, I decided.

Mushies weren't something Gordon had ready access to, but he did have plenty of speed. I was keen to try it.

The first time I did, it was a very similar experience to the mushies, but this time it lasted a lot longer. I didn't sleep for three days and two nights. It made me feel like I had the strength of the Incredible Hulk.

During the days, I carved out a track through the scrub behind our house just by using my wheelchair like a bulldozer. At night I doodled with a pen and paper, drawing the most weird and wonderful patterns and designs which didn't make any sense whatsoever.

I'd taken my first step on the path to self-destruction.

The couple of years since my divorce, leading up to this point, were a blur. Sometimes I think I was trying to fit every stupid thing that I could possibly do into as short a time as possible. I'd fully taken on the identity that went with the nickname that the boys at work had given me, "Yobbo."

One of my not so smart choices was to get friendly with one of the local bikies. Gordon had strong connections with some unsavoury characters, too, and while he never gave up the name of his drug suppliers, I suspected that's who they were.

My local pub was the Cleveland Sands, and that's where I met him. I never knew his real name, just his nickname, "Sizzler." Most of his gang hung out there, drinking and playing pool. Not being much of a gambler, I was still happy to play for a beer. I wasn't a bad pool player and won as many as I lost.

Once a week they would hold a gambling night at the clubhouse, poker or blackjack, sometimes two up. Even though I wasn't a member, I got invited to go. Maybe it was out of pity or maybe there were more sinister reasons. I'll never know.

At first, I would win a couple of bucks or break even but rarely lose. Every time I won, I got a little bit braver and bet a little more the next time. Before I knew it, I would be betting up to $100 on a single hand of cards. I started to lose more often than I would win. The longer my losing streak continued, the more they assured me my luck was about to change.

Payday at the MRD was every second Wednesday. Rocket was always the first to hear the trolley coming. "The golden eagle has landed," he'd announce. The paymaster would hand out the little brown envelopes and we would have to count it in front of him to confirm that we had received the correct amount.

Coincidentally, the card night was also on a Wednesday night. There were quite a few Thursday mornings I woke up without a cent to my name. Gambling certainly wasn't my thing.

Losing my driver's license saved me from losing my house because Gordon refused to drive me to the clubhouse.

In among my maze of booze, drugs, rock 'n' roll, gambling, and going to work to collect my pay packet, I was still looking for love. Not the "future mother of my child" kind, because that thought no longer carried much weight.

My desire was for a "fuck buddy" more than anything more serious. I was marginally better at this than I was at gambling.

I met Shirley at the Grandview hotel. She was a stunning blonde single mum, looking for the same thing that I was. Instead of the relationship we were both seeking, somehow, we "friend zoned" each other and found comfort in each other's company on the nights that neither of us got lucky, without the benefits.

There was a sexual chemistry between us, but for one reason or another, the time or the place was never right for us.

Eventually the planets aligned and I found myself naked in Shirley's bed. Actually, it was her flatmate's bed; Shirley didn't have her own. We were both a little bit drunk, but that wasn't going to stop us. After some kissing and cuddling it was finally going to happen. I was on my back, my new signature position.

Shirley was about to mount me when the door burst open. It was her flatmate, home from the pub early and obviously very randy. She stripped off her clothes and jumped on me before either of us could move. I guess if I wanted to boast about that night, I could always say it was a threesome, but Shirley didn't see much of the downstairs action. We never got another opportunity; she moved away the next week, and I never saw her again.

Sky was one of Gordon's speed customers and came by every couple of weeks. Fresh off the rebound from Shirley, I decided that Sky would be the one. All the times Sky visited our house, I never saw her snort speed with Gordon.

"That's because she shoots it," he explained. The one rule that Gordon had about his drug use was "no needles." Even though it was much more efficient that way, he never allowed anyone to use them in our house.

Here's my opportunity, I thought. What better way to get to know Sky than to take some speed around her house and shoot up together?

I got some speed off Gordon with my next pay packet and went straight around to Sky's house. I was starting to get lazy and only got out of the car when I had to, so I parked in front of her house and beeped the horn to make sure she was home first.

No one came out.

I beeped and waited for about an hour but there was no one home. The next day I called around again, beeped and waited, beeped and waited. No one home again.

I went back on the third day, but on the way there I had an unexplainable sensation which made me shiver like someone had just walked over my grave. It was a strong powerful voice in my head; if I believed in God, I would have said it was him who said, "This is not your dream. This is your worst nightmare." I was scared like I'd never been scared before.

I knew it was time to go home and let Mummy look after me for a while. I knew I would be safe there.

I had tried to live on my own in the big city, but I couldn't sustain it. After six years, I'd given it my best shot, but it wasn't good enough. I was burnt out physically, emotionally and, worst of all, I had nothing left in the think tank. I couldn't see much of a future at all.

Maybe you did need triceps to be independent.

The next day I packed everything I could fit in the back of my little Honda Civic and left the city for good. She was full right up to the roof lining, with just enough room to squeeze my wheelchair onto the passenger seat.

CHAPTER 7
ON THE FARM

The sign post said Gracemere 10 km. I drove straight past Sandy's turn off.

Sandy Small lived with her mum and dad in Gracemere, just outside Rockhampton. On the last dozen times I had driven home to visit my mum, I always called in to see her and stay overnight to break up the 1500 km trip. The term "overnight" is an under-exaggeration, if that's the opposite of exaggeration. The shortest overnight stay was three days and two nights.

Sandy loved a drink. I think that's why we got on so well. We first met in the spinal unit. She was discharged not long after my admission. We still kept in touch.

Sandy was a regular pub-goer and clubber at all the trendy spots in Rocky, and she knew where to go after hours to continue drinking.

We would always start at the Kabra pub just up the road; there was never any doubt, and we always came back for one of her mum's famous roast dinners. After that we would hit the clubs in Rockhampton until the wee hours of the morning.

While there was always a warm, clean bed in the house, I can't remember getting past the old shearers' bunk that the dogs slept on in the shed.

On one occasion, I purposely stayed an extra night at Sandy's, just so I could drive home the next day to surprise my Mum on her birthday.

"Happy birthday, Mummy!" I called out from the car as I drove in the front gate.

Mum looked up from where she was weeding her gerbera patch and calmly replied, "It was yesterday, love."

No. There would be no "overnighter" this time. I drove on through, stopping only for fuel. Most of the service stations gave full driveway service, so I didn't even have to get out of the car. One of the advantages of using a leg bag to collect your urine is you don't have to stop for a pee, either.

Since I last lived at home, Dad had moved into my room for the air conditioning but gladly relocated back to Mum's bed.

Once I'd rested for a few days to recover from my 15-hour drive, I called work to let them know what was going on. Dr Hill was happy to write a letter stating that "burnout" was common for people with spinal injuries around the 5–10-year post-injury mark. My superannuation fund paid me out a lump sum of $118,000, the equivalent of about $280,000 in today's market.

Knowing my recent track record with money, I needed to make sure I didn't piss it all up against the wall or worse. I had enough cash in the bank to set myself up for life. I knew if I fucked it up this time, I might not get another chance.

My poor little Honda Civic had served me well for six years despite the harsh treatment I gave her. A new car was top of my shopping list. Then I would need somewhere to live. Even Mum knew my move back home was only ever going to be temporary. Maybe I could find a block of land on Sandy Creek and still have enough to build a little one-bedroom cottage.

These thoughts were giving me a sense of déjà vu. All of a sudden, I realised, the dream card was back on the table, minus the wife and kids.

As far as buying cars went, I was as green as they come, but I found a demo Subaru Leone All Wheel Drive Sedan at a car yard in Townsville. The salesman said, "$14,995 on the road, $14,095 cash."

"Okay, I'll be back in an hour," I said, jumping at the saving I would be making. I could have traded the Civic and got an even better deal, but she just held too many memories to let go. She certainly did have lots of stories to tell.

I went straight to the nearest Commonwealth Bank and filled out a withdrawal slip for "Fourteen Thousand & Ninety-Five Dollars and Zero Cents." The teller put the wads of notes in a bank bag and handed it over.

The car salesman looked at me with his head tilted slightly to one side and one eyebrow cocked.

"You said 'cash'." I didn't know a bank cheque would have done the same job.

As luck would have it, a 20-acre block of land was for sale on the western bank of Sandy Creek, just five kilometres from the post office. I knew the spot intimately, I used to take my high school girlfriend there parking and tell her parents we went to the drive in.

The block had what was left of a Chinese garden from the 1870s and 24 giant mango trees, while the rest had a scattering of big old box trees. It was overrun by Chinee apple (*Ziziphus mauritiana*), an invasive plant, also introduced during the gold rush era. The old road access was badly eroded and the creek crossing had long ago been washed away in a flood. Luckily, my new Subaru was four-wheel drive. I would often get a few beers and a pie and just park under one of the box trees and let my imagination run wild.

I planned out in my head where my cottage would get built and where the shed would be.

Maybe I can still have the dream, I thought. *Maybe I can be independent and have Mum and Dad close by, just in case.*

I had turned my back on this town once already, but no one was holding onto that. I had all the support I needed right here. I just had to accept that I needed them.

My mate Tony Hicks offered to build my house for me, "mate's rates." Johnny Mara had moved away. Tony was qualified but he didn't have a builder's license, so I registered as an owner builder and used my drafting knowledge to draw up a basic set of plans for Shire council approval.

I desperately wanted to move out to the block, so the first thing to be built was a "liveable" shed. Six metres by six metres, on a concrete slab floor with corrugated iron walls and roof.

Hicksy was the master scrounger and "sourced" all the materials except the slab and roofing iron. He even found a brand-new Dover #8 wood stove that had fallen off the back of a Queensland Rail carriage. "Don't ask any questions and I won't have to lie to you," he warned.

There was no electricity or water supply connected to the block. I could make do without that luxury. Every day I came to inspect the progress and every day Tony had found another item to furnish the shed.

The shed was completed in less than a week. It had a queen-sized bed, some old antique wardrobes, a small gas fridge, the Dover, a gas camp lantern, and a stainless-steel sink connected to the rainwater tank outside. I was set up, although I still had to go to Mum and Dad's for a shower and to use the toilet.

Construction of the house started almost immediately, and Tony would arrive before daylight every day. He'd let himself in and stoke up the Dover to warm up his breakfast.

Mostly Tony worked on the house on his own, with only me to keep him company. When he needed an extra hand, I'd just go to the pub and find someone that was looking for work. Of the ten pubs in town, the Whitehorse Tavern was the best place to find a worker. Everyone got paid cash in the hand, even Tony.

There's a tradition in the building trade: once the roof is on, it has to be "wet." In other words, the boss buys a carton of beer and everyone sits around drinking and admiring their work.

Tony took this tradition a little bit further and wet everything, the foundations, the slab, the walls, the roof trusses, and the roof, of course. Every day there was something that needed to be wet.

Any time after about 5:00 pm was beer o'clock and the tools would be put down for the day. There was still no power connected, but I had the phone connected to the shed, and every night around 7:00 Tony's wife would call.

"Is Tony still there?" she'd ask.

"Tell her I've just left," he'd whisper in the background. "Tell her I've just left."

"He's just left, Kym," I'd lie. "He shouldn't be too far away."

"One more for the road and then I'll go." He never left on the first call. One drink usually meant two.

The phone would ring again in about a half an hour. I never wanted to answer it; I knew who would be calling, even without caller ID.

"Tell him to come home," Kym would say calmly, hiding her annoyance. "His dinner is cold." Somehow I don't think she liked playing this nightly game as much as Tony.

During the next few months, work on the house continued without too many setbacks. Tony even managed to find some coloured split face blocks just like the ones I had pictured years earlier. I eventually got the power connected. It had to come from about a kilometre away and the cost was a lot higher than I'd anticipated.

I still had no reliable water supply. The average rainfall would never be enough to supply a household. After an anxious few days, I managed to find a water diviner who found a good supply and sank a bore into it. The water wasn't very good quality, but at least I would be able to shower and not have to go to Mum and Dad's every day.

Final inspection day arrived and the building inspector gave us his approval. My cottage was complete. All up, it had only cost me a little under $80,000, including the land. There was still work to do on the block, but I had my home and a place to live

As a house warming present, Tony arranged for one of his mates who worked for the city council to leave a small bulldozer on the block. Over the next few days he cleaned up the access road, cleared some fence lines, and pushed a small dam in the middle of the block.

In my school days vision, I had a small Brahma stud. Twenty acres of this country wouldn't even hold one cow, let alone a stud. My sister, Suzie Brodie, and her husband Gary had a cattle property just outside town. Centauri holding was 11,000 acres, and even that was considered small.

Gary's brother, Wayne, had recently returned to the property after his own adventures in the big smoke. Some of which we shared. One day I was out there visiting and his dad said, "You need to get some Angora goats on your little block. There's good money in Mohair and they'll clean up all that Chinee apple in no time."

While Centauri was small, it was still big enough to source all the fence posts and rails I needed. Centauri was also the hub for the Brodie family, and they rallied around to help me fence my block. Gary, Wayne, Steve, and uncles Albert and Jim worked from daylight till dark for a couple of weeks at my place to make it "goat proof." They never once asked for anything in return.

I bought some goats from one of the pioneers of the Angora industry in Australia, Alma Bode, and before I knew it, I was a goat farmer.

I really took the bull (goat) by the horns. I bought top quality Angora goats from some of the best stud breeders in Queensland and joined the Angora Mohair Breeders Association. I set up a one-man shearing stand in the shed.

Being cattle country, it was difficult to find a shearer, but eventually I tracked one down. Bill was an accountant but jumped at the opportunity to get the narrow blade in his hands again. He had kept his gear from his days in the shearing sheds around Richmond. His going rate was one stubby per goat, and consequently I only ever got three or four shorn at a time.

My stud breeding program went well and I started to exhibit my animals at agricultural shows across North Queensland. This was the perfect way to be competitive again, without the hard work and training. I won grand champion ribbons at most of the shows I attended, but that's the only place I was successful.

The bottom fell out of the mohair market and there was no way they could ever become a viable business. Even so, there was no way I was going to give them up. Around about the same time, a new breed of goats was imported into Australia, South African Boer goats. They were beautiful and bred for their meat, just like Brahma cattle. They become my new hobby, my interest, my passion. Waking up in the early hours of the morning to hear a newly born kiddie goat crying like a baby is one of life's most magical sounds.

Never being allowed to have a dog as a child, one of the first things I did when I moved out to the block was get myself a puppy.

My first dog was a stumpy tailed blue cattle dog I named Koona, because I "koona" think of a better name. Everywhere I went, Koona went. She was most comfortable under my wheelchair, even when I was moving.

One day when we had gone in to town to get some groceries, Koona took up her usual spot underneath me. I never had to worry about her under there; I knew she was safe and, most of all, not getting into trouble.

As we left the supermarket to put the groceries in the car, I heard a loud screech of skidding car tyres, followed almost immediately by a dull thud!

Shit. Someone's just been run over on the pedestrian crossing. I had to drop the grocery bags in the boot before I could turn around to see what had happened.

I couldn't believe what I saw.

"I'm so sorry," the young woman apologised sincerely, "he just came from nowhere."

"She," I snapped, correcting her. Koona lay motionless in the middle of Gill Street, the main street in town.

For some unknown reason, she'd ran out onto the road and was hit and killed instantly.

I started crying like a baby. She didn't have a mark on her, not even a drop of blood. This was the first time I could remember ever crying in public, and thinking back now, it must have been the accumulation of emotions from the last eight years.

Starting with my spinal injury cutting me down before I even had a chance to start my dream, getting up again and working towards my new dream in Brisbane only to have it cut down again – and now, with the pieces of my latest vision finally starting to fall into place, I was knocked back down again.

I took her back to the farm, went out into the paddock under the shade of a big box tree, and dug a grave. It was not an easy thing for me to do, physically or emotionally, but it was something I needed to do as part of the process. I sat under the tree and cried until I had no more tears left, and then I said goodbye to my beautiful little friend.

I never thought about replacing her. How can you replace your first love? But about six months later, one of my goat breeder friends called me to say she had a pup she wanted me to have. I hadn't seen her in ages, so I took the opportunity to drive to Mackay to visit and to tell her in person I wasn't ready for another dog.

Polly was the runt of the litter. One side of her face was white, the other side black, like she was two different dogs. She was. She came straight up to me and looked up into my eyes with a smile which just melted my heart. There was an instant connection, like love at first sight.

Maybe I could love another dog?

I changed my mind on the spot.

We put her on the floor in front of the back seat and as I drove away, she started to whine and scratch at the back of my seat. *Oh crap! What have I just done?* The next thing I knew, she was on the console beside me. She stopped crying, looked up at me with the most trusting eyes, put her head on my leg, and fell fast asleep. That's where she stayed for the next five hours until we arrived back at the farm.

Everybody loved Polly, even Dad.

Even though Dad never understood why I wanted to live on a farm or breed goats, he would always help me whenever I asked him. He'd built up a rapport with Hicksy during the construction of the cottage and loved to visit at beer o'clock to tell us his yarns and dirty jokes or show us the latest thing he'd built. He should have been a cabinet maker instead of a clerk; his craftsmanship was superb.

I found that if I asked him to do anything, even though he'd agree, he would complain the whole time – work like a slave but whinge like a spoilt brat. "Stupid fucking goats, stupid fucking farm. Why would you want to live way out here?" When it was his idea, though, it was completely different. I learnt how to plant the seed to make it his idea.

"Have you seen all that bellyache bush coming up along the creek, Dad?" I'd throw the bait. "I'll have to hire someone to come and slash it before it takes over the place." I knew slashing wouldn't control it.

"Slashing's no good, you've gotta pull it out by the roots. I'll come and have a look tomorrow if I get time."

The next day before dawn, I would hear his Toyota driving along the creek bank. By the time I got up and showered, he would have the tray full of bellyache bush. I'd call him up for lunch and then he'd go back and work until dark without a single complaint.

Once the house was built and all the fencing was done, it got kind of lonely on the farm. Mum's brothers worked shift work, and I knew most days one of them would be having a beer at the St Patrick's Hotel, so I started frequenting there to have a beer and play pool. They were arguably the best two pool players in town, and the young blokes all wanted to knock them off their perch. Playing for beers, I teamed up with them to play doubles and rarely needed to get my wallet out.

On Saturday mornings, the footy club held their meat tray raffles at the White Horse Tavern. This was a trap I struggled to avoid. Most Saturdays I'd do my grocery shopping and only go into the tavern to "support" the club. I quickly learnt not to buy any cold or frozen groceries, because it was usually melted by the time I left the Tavern.

The local cops were lenient on drink driving unless you were an arsehole about it. They'd drive around the pubs and check out whose cars were parked outside. If you stayed too long, they'd come in and tell you to get a lift home. They knew Uncle Tom and Uncle John well. My car was parked in the supermarket car park so it wouldn't look like I'd been at the pub all morning.

I'd left the Tavern on one of these Saturdays and was in a rush to get my groceries home. I'd passed my DD test and was driving home a bit faster than I should, taking the back streets just in case. Losing control of the car on a gravel road, I slid sideways into the table drain.

The car flipped completely, landing back on its wheels off to the side of the road.

From the moment I lost control, it was like slow motion. Time seemed to almost stop. At one point as the car was completely upside down all the loose coins from the console seemed to be hanging in the air like I was inside a spaceship in zero gravity.

I wasn't hurt, but I couldn't open the door or get my wheelchair out. Luckily someone came along only a minute later and was able to open the door, get my wheelchair out, and help me to get out. I was just up the road from Hicksy's place, so I pushed myself there as fast as I could. I didn't want the cops to put me on the breathalyser again.

As soon as I arrived, I got Kym to call the police. Then I skulled three cans of Fosters lager and wished that Polly was there so I could lick her arse to get the taste out of my mouth. I don't know anyone else in the world who likes the taste of Fosters. Three cans would put me over the limit even if I hadn't been drinking all morning. That was my plan to avoid a drink driving charge once the police arrived.

Senior Sergeant Dennis Weildon arrived with a junior constable.

"What happened, Col?" he asked in his formal policeman style.

"I was driving a bit too quick and lost control on the dirt," I replied.

"Both passenger side tires are flat, I think you had a blowout," he said, giving me the perfect reason for the accident.

"No, Dennis," I countered, "pretty sure I was just driving too quick."

The Constable went to get the ticket book out and Dennis put his hand on his shoulder to stop him.

"YOU HAD A BLOW OUT!" the Sarge repeated.

"No, I don't think so…" I started, but he didn't let me finish.

"The official police report says you had a blowout."

"Oh yes," I said, finally. "That must've been what happened, then."

Dennis's car was often parked for long periods behind the Sovereign Hotel when he wasn't on duty. I think that might explain his leniency. Or maybe he felt sorry for me. Either way, I didn't go to jail that time.

With ten pubs in town competing with each other for business, they all had their point of difference. The railway workers drank at the Enterprise, the Crown catered more for the business sector, the footballers were at the Tavern, the livestock and real estate agents were at the Sovereign, and the rodeo riders drank at the Waverley.

The Saint Patrick's hotel became my local, which was not that logical given it was the furthest from my home. It had a loyal following of locals and itinerants. Their social club held regular pool competitions and fixtures on the pub's tennis court. It had a real family feel, and Maria was the best pub cook in town.

There was always a good crowd there on the weekends. The Pats, as we liked to call it, attracted not only lots of patrons but also lots of hawkers. Anyone with a raffle ticket to sell or a cause to raise money for would do the rounds of the pubs.

Anne Franzmann was dressed in a Sid costume, the Slip, Slop, Slap Seagull, helping her friend, Anthea, raise funds for skin cancer research.

"Nice breasts for a seagull." My pickup lines were still chronically cheesy and met with the same level of indifference.

Just when I thought she was about to say "Why, thank you," give me a wink, and ask me to take her out on a date, she turned and walked away.

Anne was a teacher at St Mary's College for Catholic girls and lived in the teachers' house opposite the school.

It was there I met her the second time.

After that, we seemed to run into each other everywhere. Her friends had the same friends as some of mine. Most of our mutual friends were couples, and it wasn't long before the two of us got together as a couple.

Before long, we were spending most of our spare time together.

On the weekends, she would sleep over at my cottage and get up early in the morning to return to the school house. Her nocturnal habits didn't go unnoticed by the senior staff at her school, and while they never said as much, she knew it was frowned upon. Moving into my place and "living in sin" wouldn't be a suitable option, either.

It seemed the best way to keep everyone happy was to get married.

Yesterday Today Tomorrow

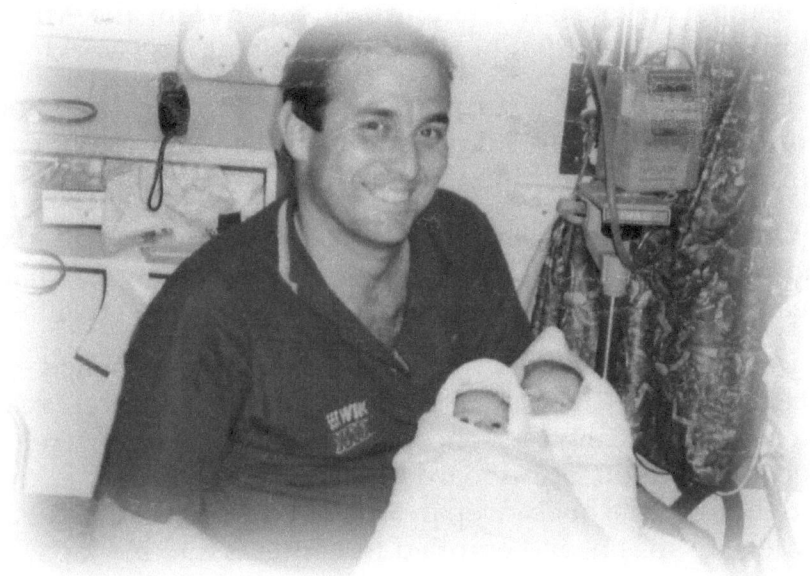

CHAPTER 8

LIFE AND DEATH

With Anne at work all week, I soon learned that my understanding of a 9 to 3 school teaching job wasn't the reality at all.

Working in a private school, the teachers had much higher expectations placed on them. They were expected not only to teach their classes during school hours but also to participate in after-school activities. There always seemed to be an athletics carnival or a netball match or a school concert which kept Anne back most nights until at least 6 o'clock.

Staying at home watching the goats grow or watching daytime soaps on TV got the better of me. I had to find something to do. Since taking my super from the MRD, I hadn't given any thought to getting back into the workforce.

The boredom was turning me back into a yobbo. Some mornings I didn't get out of bed until after Anne had gone to work. Sometimes I didn't even do that.

One morning I rolled out of bed, too lethargic to have a shower or get dressed. I just slipped on a dressing gown and meandered into the kitchen to make myself some breakfast.

I wasn't a great cook, but I was pretty good at boiled eggs on toast. The toaster had just popped and the eggs were ready to come off. Lifting the saucepan off the hotplate, I carefully placed it onto the breadboard on my lap. As I turned to carry it to the sink, the hot saucepan touched my bare belly, causing my legs to spasm, and emptied its contents into my lap.

"OH FUCK!" Even though I couldn't feel it, I screamed in shock, knowing that if I could feel it the pain would be excruciating. I raced straight into the bathroom and got under the shower. Briefly getting out to call an ambulance, I returned to the shower and that's where they found me when they arrived.

The newly boiled water had run down through my groin on both sides and lay in a pool underneath my bum. Everything in between was cooked.

I'd done a good job: third degree burns, which would require a six-week stay in hospital.

There's a funny side to every story. Not that I found it particularly funny at the time, but when I lifted the cloche off my evening meal that first night in hospital, there staring back at me were Cheerios and baked beans. A little red sausage with the skin peeling back off the end.

"You're fucking kidding me!" I looked around to see if one of my nurse friends were watching for my reaction. They weren't. Jamie Oliver obviously wasn't doing the catering at this hospital.

I was left with some really serious scars, not that I could ever get them out at the pub when the boys were having one of those "my scar is bigger than yours" show and tell games. I never liked that game much anyway. The thought of another drunk bloke lifting his shirt up to show me his scars and tell me "I was in a wheelchair once" sends a chill up my spine.

Less than a month later, I broke my femur and spent another six weeks in hospital, this time in the Townsville Base Hospital. More serious scars that will never see the light of day. I couldn't wait to get out and get back to the job hunt.

Even though I was entitled to a disability pension, I joined the Job Club at Skillshare. I'd only ever applied for one job before, so this was all new territory for me. My computer skills were non-existent, so that was the first thing I had to do. I put myself through a basic computer course at TAFE.

I tried a few different jobs before I found one which ticked all the boxes. Physically doable, paid well, and gave me a sense of purpose.

Hicksy's dad owned the Mitre 10 store and gave me a job making pine lattice work, but it was just a little bit beyond my physical capabilities.

I did the books for one of the local butchers, but his trade wasn't strong enough to keep us both in work.

Anne got me some work at her school tutoring the indigenous kids from Palm Island and running the outdoor Ed camps. I was always good at maths at school, and once word got out that I was doing home tutoring, a few people asked me to tutor their kids.

I got some volunteer work on the Charters Towers Show Committee, and once a year I volunteered at the Goldfield Ashes Cricket Carnival, arguably the biggest organised social cricket carnival in the Southern Hemisphere.

It still wasn't enough. I needed a full-time job.

That job eventually came in the form of the administration assistant at a specialist disability employment agency, Dalflin Employment. We were a double income, no-kids family, unless you counted the baby goats as kids. We had dozens of them.

It was time to start a real family. I hoped that my boiling water trick hadn't ruined my chances in the downstairs department.

During the next school holidays, we made an appointment to see Dr Hill and flew to Brisbane to meet with him and Queensland Fertility Group (QFG) specialist Dr David Molloy.

The little room at the PA was just the same as the last time I was in it, and the vibrator looked just as sinister as it had that first time. We got the same result: a retrograde ejaculation and a blood pressure peak over 200.

This time we didn't look at the semen through Vernon's microscope. We rushed it straight to the QFG clinic to get their scientists to evaluate it.

While we were there, Anne went through some examinations to ensure there were no fertility issues on her side. Everything looked good, and our chances for a pregnancy were as good as anyone undergoing the same fertility program.

Dr Molloy explained the options to us and advised us on which one he thought had the best chance of success. One of his nurses walked us through the nightmare of paperwork that we would have to plough through. The paperwork would be nothing compared to what Anne would be going through. This was not the way she pictured starting a family, either.

Gamete intrafallopian transfer, more commonly referred to as the GIFT procedure, was the way we would make our baby. We hoped.

Over the course of the next six weeks, Anne took fertility drugs to stimulate egg production in her ovaries.

Nearing the end of that time, we had to drive back to Brisbane for Dr Molloy to monitor the growth of the ovarian follicles. We would be in Brisbane for the last week and would need a car to get around, so flying down wasn't an option.

Dad travelled with us to give Anne her injections during the trip. Neither of us had the dexterity to administer them in the place they needed to go. Thirty-six hours before the egg "pick up," Anne was injected with human chorionic gonadotropin (hCG). The egg pick-up was done under general anaesthetic.

Up until this point, only Anne had personally experienced the highs and the lows of the hormone-induced emotions. I just had to tippy toe around the eggshells, making sure I didn't do or say anything which would trigger her. Now I had to cope with the anxiety of my wife going under and the risks involved with any general anaesthetic.

Please let her come out of it. I smoked and paced up and down Wickham Terrace outside the Saint Andrews private hospital for what seemed like an eternity.

My stomach was in knots, the effect of smoking too many cigarettes and not having anything to eat or drink. Then, while she was in recovery, the wait for Dr Molloy to tell me if there were any viable eggs. *Please, please let there be some. Oh, what if there's none?*

Apart from the stress on us both and the physical toll on Anne's body, there was the financial cost. A full GIFT cycle cost us about $1500 out of our own pockets. Travel and accommodation were on top of that.

Then it was my turn. QFG didn't offer the service I needed to collect my semen, so I had to get that done at the Princess Alexandra hospital and then rush it back to St Andrews to be washed and prepped. On my previous visits to Dr Hill, I wasn't really under any great pressure to deliver. This time, the conception of my child depended on it. This time, the continuation of the "Mackereth" family name depended on it.

Vernon was his usual, calm, "absent-minded professor" self and executed his part with expert precision. Tucking my little specimen jar into my pocket, I sped back to Spring Hill. *The cops better not try to pull me over, because I ain't stopping.*

The final step in the GIFT procedure was to place my sperm, and Anne's eggs, back into her fallopian tubes using a laparoscope and let nature take its course.

We had discussed the likelihood of a pregnancy if we used one, two, or the maximum of three eggs. The probability of it being a multiple pregnancy was high if we went with more than one. We opted for three; we wanted the odds to be as high as possible.

Then came the wait. The longest two weeks of my life. The wait to watch the little line on the home pregnancy test turn into a cross before our eyes.

As luck and fate would have it, we weren't the only couple in the area going through the same procedure. I wasn't the only person with a spinal injury trying to start a family. There was another couple living in Townsville, just 140 km away.

Not long before I met Anne, Johnny Beare called me out of the blue. After some small talk he said, "My next-door neighbour has had a motorbike accident and has just come home from the spinal unit. He's not coping so well; would you mind giving him a call?"

"Yeah, sure," I said. That call to Peter Allen was the start of a great friendship.

Anne and I spent lots of time visiting him and his wife Dawn. I shared my experience living with a spinal injury and we had interesting, sometimes vigorous, discussions about everything from religion to politics over beers and a BBQ. Just like us, Peter and Dawn wanted to start a family, and they went through their first GIFT cycle only a week before ours.

We were the first people they called to hear their good news. In another week, we would be returning their call with our own good news. Neither of us slept the night before; we were far too excited.

The best time to do the pregnancy test was first thing in the morning, and I waited eagerly outside the toilet door for Anne to come out waving the positive test with joy.

She was taking too long; something wasn't right, I knew before she came out that the test was negative. The expression on her face was hard to describe. It was a mixture of sadness, grief, and failure. I had no words to comfort her, just as I had no positive thoughts to comfort myself.

"We'll try again." My words did nothing for either of us, and she went into the bathroom to shower and get ready for work.

It's strange how all of a sudden you notice things that previously you didn't. Everywhere we went there were pregnant women. Everywhere we went there seemed to be young kids with unwanted pregnancies, and here we were desperate to give our child the best upbringing possible. If only it were that easy for us.

We tried again. Another six weeks of hormones. Another drive to Brisbane. Another anxious wait for Anne to come out of theatre. Another rushed trip from the PA to Saint Andrews. Another 1500 km trip home. Another $1500 – not that we cared about the money. We would have paid a million if we could.

Another two weeks of the cruellest and drawn-out wait for that positive test.

Another negative.

We tried a third time, and a fourth. By now we were old hat at this. By now we were hardened to the gut-wrenching sadness that came with each negative test. And by now my expectations were very low, and I was prepared for the negative result that I was sure would come again.

"It's positive," Anne whispered from behind the toilet door.

I think we were both in too much shock at the result to get excited. I remembered Mum's words again: "Don't get your hopes up too high, love."

"I'll feel a lot better after you've had a blood test," I said. I was trying to protect Anne in the same way Mum was trying to protect me.

The blood test came back positive, but I still wouldn't allow myself the luxury of getting too excited. If we were conceiving naturally, Anne wouldn't even know if she'd missed a period at this point. Besides, everyone knew it was bad luck to announce your pregnancy before the 12-week mark. That day came and went, and we were still pregnant. It was only then that I started to feel good about becoming a parent for the first time.

The first scan would truly put any residual doubt to rest. I will never forget the first time I heard the oosh d oosh d oosh sound of my unborn baby's heart beat and the unstoppable tears of joy and relief that came with it.

"Listen, can you hear that?" the radiographer asked.

"Yeah, it sounds like an echo." I could hear it faintly.

"That's not an echo," she said. "It's another baby. Let's see if we can pick it up better over here." She squeezed another large dollop of gel on the other side of Anne's tummy.

Oosh d oosh d oosh.

"There it is alright," she said, picking up another heartbeat. "Congratulations, you're having twins."

We followed the growth of our babies in one of the many pregnancy books Anne had bought. I learned about trimesters and everything else I needed to know about pregnancy. We had already made it safely through the first trimester.

We ticked off the weeks of the second trimester, 13, 14, 15…and with the passing of each week, we became more and more at ease that we would make it all the way to 40 weeks. With twins, it would be more like 36 weeks.

Life and Death

…22, 23, 24. Everything was on track.

We took a road trip to Mackay to attend a friend's wedding. "I've got a bit of a cramp in the tummy" Anne said as she got out of the car. Neither of us were too concerned. We assumed it was from sitting in the same position for five hours straight. The next morning, she had some spotting. We'd both read the books and knew that wasn't so unusual and only cause for alarm if it got heavier. It did. We made an appointment to see our gynaecologist the next day.

Anne was admitted into the Mater Private hospital in Townsville; she was going into premature labour at 24 weeks. She was given drugs to stop or slow down her labour. "If we can't stop you from going into labour before 30 weeks, you'll have to be transferred over to the Kirwan." The public hospital had a neonatal care unit.

These impatient little buggers had already decided they were coming, now. On 3 September 1993, Anne gave birth to Kate and Veronica in the Kirwan Women's Hospital.

They looked perfect. Tiny miniatures of full-term babies, weighing less than 600 grams each. While they appeared perfect on the outside, their lungs and other organs were still seriously underdeveloped. They were immediately placed in incubators. They were both in seriously critical condition.

My emotions were in conflict. I wanted to shout out to the world "LOOK WHAT WE MADE!" but I couldn't do that yet. I was in a state of shock and disbelief.

I wanted to protect my babies from the perilous danger they were confronted with, but I could do nothing. When I'd first realised that my hands would never be able to grasp anything firmly again, I felt useless, but this was worse, much worse.

The doctors gave them little chance of surviving, but each day they lived, their chances improved. Over the next two days, countless doctors, nurses, and specialists explained to us the treatments they were giving our babies and what effect those treatments might have. They might as well have been speaking in a foreign language. I was in shock and could only stare at them through the Perspex of the incubator, oblivious to what was going on around me.

The neonatal unit had limited accommodation for parents, none of which was wheelchair accessible. After two days without showering or toileting and sleeping in my car in the carpark, Anne said, "Go home, you stink." I reluctantly went home to shower, shave, and use my toilet.

On my return the next day, I was confronted by a chaotic scene. Veronica, the youngest, had deteriorated overnight. She was taken away for a brain scan, but when she came back, the mood of the treating team had darkened. "She's not going to make it." This time I heard the doctor loud and clear. "Her brain is just too badly damaged."

"She will pass within minutes of us taking her out of the incubator," he said, reaffirming my deepest fears. "If you like, you can hold her until she goes." There was a special room just down the corridor specifically set up for parents to spend the last minutes of their child's life in private. We took Veronica there and held her while we both sobbed uncontrollably.

We stayed there for about half an hour. I couldn't say I felt her go but she had stopped breathing, and we knew we had to go back to her sister's side. We took Veronica to say goodbye to Kate in spirit and then one of the nurses took her from us.

Once again, we were conflicted. We wanted to grieve the loss of our baby girl but knew we had to stay strong for her sister who was fighting as hard as she could to beat almost unbeatable odds.

Holding in my sorrow, I spoke to the doctor about what I needed to do to make the funeral arrangements. I never had to bury anyone before. This was undoubtedly the worst day of my life – but it was about to get even worse.

"No need to rush that," he said.

"What do you mean 'no need to rush'?" There was something about his demeanour that didn't sit well with me.

"It's best to wait and bury them both together."

I was dumbfounded by his response. I could feel my blood starting to boil and rage rise up from the pit of my stomach. How could someone be that cold-hearted about the death of a child and talk so matter-of-factly about another whose life was hanging in the balance?

I wanted to grab him by the throat and rip his cold fucking heart out of his chest.

Up until this point, I had been in denial about the most likely fate of my babies. Now I was angry. I knew I had a bad temper, but never before had it been directed at a person. Someone had to be blamed. Someone had to be held to account. I took a minute to compose myself.

I looked him squarely in the eyes and said sternly, "I'm taking my baby home to bury her!"

One of Dad's mates was the undertaker in Charters Towers. Dad had nicknamed him "Boxer." Strangely, I no longer saw the humour in it. Veronica's coffin was tiny yet as beautiful as her, white with lace trimmings. Her graveside service was one of the biggest I'd ever seen, yet she had never even met one of her mourners. In such a short space of time, my beautiful baby girl brought a whole community together.

Not to be outdone, just over a fortnight later her twin sister gave an encore performance, and now they lie together, resting in peace.

Yesterday Today Tomorrow

CHAPTER 9

LIVING THE DREAM

For months I was trapped in the anger of my grief. I needed someone to blame for stealing my future happiness.

I wanted to blame Anne, but I knew it wasn't her fault.

I wanted to blame the school for putting her under so much stress.

I wanted to blame the lazy teachers who never carried any of the after-school load. I knew stress was a major contributing factor to premature labour.

I wanted to blame our friends for inviting us to a wedding so far away.

I wanted to blame myself for allowing any of those things to happen… But it wasn't my fault, either.

I wanted to blame God for cruelly bringing someone into this world, only to choose them to be angels before they had a chance to learn their life lessons.

While the death of our daughters was a devastating blow, we never gave up on our dream. We got back on the IVF rollercoaster. Medicare would fund six IVF cycles in total. We had two chances left. After that we would have to pay the total cost.

Our fifth attempt was just like the previous ones, only this time we went into it a lot more battle-hardened and prepared for any outcome. After what we'd gone through, we could cope with anything. Nothing could be worse that the living hell of the last year. We were right back where we started.

By now Anne had figured out how to give herself the fertility injections, so we didn't tell anyone we were trying again.

Still holding onto the anger and emptiness of my loss, I expressed no emotion when Anne showed me the negative pregnancy test result. At least we didn't have to answer the same question a hundred times. "So, how did you go?" and answer with just a dejected look and a shake of the head and wait for the "Next time you will." Force a tight-lipped grin and without any conviction say, "Sure, next time."

With every cycle so far, there had been no issues with the quality of Anne's eggs or my semen. They were as good as anyone's, probably better than most.

The procedures had all gone perfectly. Eggs, semen, in the fallopian tube together, how much easier could it be to conceive? I couldn't understand why we didn't get pregnant every time and yet one of our friends fell while she was on the pill. It didn't make sense.

There's a saying, "Lucky last." I didn't believe in luck, but at the same time, I hoped more than anything that our last attempt would be lucky. Yet, I still stared in disbelief at the cross on the last test. I still had no emotion to express. I was in "self-protection" mode.

Anne was pregnant again.

The weeks passed even more slowly than they had with the girls. Our first scan revealed that we were having twins again. Bitter and sweet news. Bitter in that it increased the chances of another premature labour, but sweet in that we would have our family in one go if we made it through to full term. The odds had just lengthened.

We got to the end of the first trimester and people started to notice, but nobody asked the question they all wanted to ask. We let our family and close friends in on the secret, but in small country towns there are no secrets.

Eventually the second trimester came to an end and we entered uncharted territory, at least for us.

After 30 weeks, I felt a weight lifted off my shoulders. Even if Anne went into labour now, the chances of the babies surviving were quite good. That was how I measured each passing week: not by how big they were according to the books, but by their chances of survival if they came today. My history with gambling was poor.

At one point we went for a routine scan and the radiographer, without thinking, said, "This one's a boy."

"We don't want to know!" we said at the same time.

I already knew we were having a "pigeon pair," anyway, one boy and one girl. So, she hadn't really told me anything new. I had a feeling in my gut.

At 36 weeks, Anne was enormous. She was really uncomfortable, but other than constantly getting kicked in the bladder, everything was normal and healthy.

By the time she reached 38 weeks, everyone wanted them out. We went back to the birthing suites at the Kirwan Women's.

The birth was progressing just like the textbooks. Anne wasn't the "hand-holdy" type, so the last thing she needed was me clinging on to her. I got the front row seat, literally, down at the business end. Even though we'd watched the videos in prenatal classes, I wasn't prepared for what I was about to see.

My baby boy was the first to come and presented perfectly.

I can't remember how long the labour lasted. Anne would, I'm sure. I can't imagine her pain.

The birth was textbook. The nurse asked me if I wanted to cut the umbilical cord, but I didn't have enough function in my hands. My emotions were all over the place at that moment. I was on such a high and yet I couldn't help thinking about Kate and Veronica. I watched as they wrapped him in what looked like a towel and passed him to his mother to hold.

"Twin two is coming," someone announced.

My baby girl was on the way.

For the past few months, we had been throwing around names, I wanted Thomas and Gemima. I can't remember the names Anne liked, but after witnessing their birth and what she went through, I gave up all naming rights.

"This one is breech." The midwife prepared the team for a more complicated than normal birth.

As far as breech births go, this one was textbook, too. My focus was fixed on my baby girl making her way into the world.

The first part of her to see the light of day was her testicles.

I was gutted.

Not because we had another boy – that concept wasn't even in my head – but because my little girl was deformed.

The penny hadn't dropped that this baby was also a boy. My gut tightened, my heart sank, and I started to get a lump in my throat.

Why is this happening to me? My mind was racing. I knew what it was like to live with a disability, and I didn't want my little girl to go through what I had.

"Two healthy little boys," the midwife congratulated us. "You've both done really well."

"Wait! What? What did you just say?" I was really confused.

"You've got twin boys," she said.

Oh, my God. A wave of relief washed over me. I was such an idiot.

The firstborn we named Joseph Colin, as was the family tradition, taking his father's Christian name as his middle name. His younger brother by 14 minutes, we named Benjamin Vernon after Dr Vernon Hill, without whom we would not have been able to have children.

That's about where the formalities ended. After only a couple of days, we took Joey and Benno home.

Strangely, my four-legged best friend Polly moved herself out of the house the same day and never came inside again unless there was thunder or gunshots, and then she would sneak back in and hide under the bed. Somehow, she sensed that the dynamics of the household had changed.

She became very protective of the boys, and while she was never aggressive, she would always position herself between them and any danger which might threaten them.

At last, we had started our family. After two years of triumphs and tragedies, we had finally done it.

We'd done it, all right, but we hadn't really thought through the reality of looking after twins. On the other hand, we didn't know any different, so we had nothing to compare to. Unlike most couples, sharing the parenting responsibilities would look a lot different at our place.

Anne was determined to breastfeed for as long as she possibly could, which sounds all well and good until you try to feed two babies at the same time.

While in the hospital, we were shown the "football hold," a technique for holding two babies to breastfeed at the same time. The name in itself was a very accurate description, as the babies were tucked under Anne's armpit like a footballer would hold a football.

This is a fantastic technique if both babies feed at the same time and the same speed. That was never the case, and it seemed that for at least 20 hours of every day, there was at least one baby attached to Anne's breast. Many times, I would wake up during the night to find her asleep on the couch with one baby asleep under one arm and the other wide awake, chewing on her nipple.

I was unable to help; apart from the obvious lack of mammary glands, I wasn't able to physically help her much, either. About all I could do was make the occasional cup of coffee.

Anne struggled through the first six weeks severely sleep deprived, only managing to get an hour here or an hour there. Never more than two straight. The decision to put them on the bottle couldn't have come sooner for her.

Now it was my turn to share some of the load. Anne could finally get a little bit of respite. I still wasn't a huge help, but I could at least give one baby his bottle after Anne had prepared it all and set me up.

We managed to get them into a routine, where they both had their bottles at the same time. We would swap around a little bit so that sometimes I would feed Benno while Anne fed Joey and other times it would be the reverse.

It was my sole responsibility to put them to bed. Instead of the traditional nursery rhymes or bedtime stories, I read them poetry by Henry Lawson or Banjo Paterson, or sang a Seekers or Rolf Harris song. They loved "Mulga Bill's Bicycle."

They always seemed to wake up at about 3 am for a feed. I would get myself out of bed and into my wheelchair while Anne got the bottles ready. She would put a pillow on my lap, give me one of the babies and a bottle, then turn the TV on and settle back into bed with the other one.

Trying to find something to watch on TV at that hour of the day was the greatest challenge, and most times we settled for a rerun of *Cop Shop*. Unfortunately, *Cop Shop* would finish before the boys finished their bottles, and then we were stuck watching whatever program came on after that. It was an old TV and didn't have a remote control. We unwillingly watched a lot of Kenneth Copeland, the American TV evangelist.

We made the decision that we wouldn't use disposable nappies. Luckily, my sister Katrina was a fashion designer with Bonds babywear and would send us huge bundles of baby clothes and lots and lots of cloth nappies. Changing nappies was another job I didn't have the function to be able to do. What a shame.

So, I never changed a single nappy. My job was washing, drying, and folding them, ready for Anne to use.

Forty nappies a day. I scraped the shit out of them. I soaked them. I put a load in the washing machine and hung a load out to dry every morning before I left for work. I did the same every afternoon as soon as I got home and again before I went to bed each night.

By the time the boys were six months old, Ben had learned how to climb out of his cot and into our bed during the night. My family had outgrown my one-bedroom cottage. The boys needed their own room. We engaged Hicksy's services again and built an extension on the house.

My quaint little cottage got transformed into a family home. A room each for the boys, a huge living area, another bathroom and toilet, and a bullnose veranda around three sides. We moved them into one of the rooms together.

Everything was starting to look like my high school dream, or an equally acceptable variation of it, had become reality.

It had a 20-acre patch on Sandy Creek.

It had a split face Besser block home; hell, it even had his and hers bathrooms.

It had a wife, two kids, and a dog.

It had a full-time job and some part time "teaching" work.

It had two cars in the shed. One was a Toyota Dual cab Hi Lux – not quite the GXL cruiser.

It had a 410 shotgun and a .22 rifle locked in the gun safe.

It had a goat stud and even had a sign post on the turn off from the highway, "Blackjack Boers." Our road was named "Mackereth Road" after me, and the shire council erected a sign post for that, too.

I had a clothesline out the back and a veranda out the front, with lots of socialising and good times with friends and family.

We were living the dream.

For ten years, we lived the dream.

CHAPTER 10

SOMETHING'S MISSING

For ten years, I lived a dream.

I watched my kids growing up. Their first day at preschool. Their second day, when Benno protested, "we already did that yesterday." He was always looking for something new to discover.

I dropped them off at school and picked them up in the afternoons.

Took them to soccer for a season, rugby league for a season, cricket for a season. They didn't have a great love of sport. They mostly just enjoyed being with the other kids.

When one of their schoolmates asked them to join his dance troop, I didn't think they'd go for it, but they did. It was such a great bunch of boys that they went back and danced for three more years.

There were lots of other kids living in the area, and most weekends they would meet at the creek crossing and amuse themselves for hours. They usually all ended back at our place looking for a feed. Joey would often bring home a new "pet" he had caught: small fish or crabs or insects he would keep in jars under his bed.

Most of the other kids had motor bikes. I promised my boys if they saved up their money, I'd go halves with them in a Pee Wee 50. All their pocket money and birthday money went into an old cake tin. Every night they would get out the money tin, spread out all the notes and coins, sort them out, and add up the total, even if they hadn't added to it.

"Can we go out to visit Dar tomorrow?" they'd ask. Their great-grandfather was always willing to help the cause and would give them a $50 note for their tin.

"You boys really love Dar, don't you?" I'd tease them. I knew they knew I knew why the sudden interest in visiting him.

They helped me around the farm, but while they loved the goats, they never developed the passion I had for them. Sometimes we'd go away for a show and camp overnight at the Showgrounds. Bush kids learn to pull their weight at an early age. My boys took on responsibilities well before most of their school buddies. They quickly got used to getting up before dawn when we went on a road trip.

Wayne Brodie secretly loved the goats, not that he ever admitted it to his "cattle cocky" mates. He would always come to help us. We had our regular fuel stops along the way.

Something's Missing

On one particular trip, we had stopped at a roadhouse just outside Clermont.

"You filling up here?" Wayne asked while I stayed in the car.

"Yeah," I said. The boys both got out of the car to check the goats in the trailer.

Benno came back and took my credit card, I assumed for Wayne to use.

Five minutes later he jumped back in the front seat with a packet of Maltesers.

"How did you pay for that?" I asked him. He held up the credit card; his mouth was too full to answer

PayWave wasn't a thing then; you were required to sign for your purchases on the receipt.

"But you needed to sign," I said. He held up the receipt with the letters BEN, written in his 6-year-old handwriting.

They were growing up so quickly.

I travelled all over the state exhibiting the goats at agricultural shows and field days. It was a great combination of my love of driving and my passion to promote the goat industry.

I drove to the Sydney Royal Easter Show every year for six years without ever winning a ribbon. It was over 4000 km round trip just to compare my animals with the best in the country. More often than not I'd return home with more goats than I took after bidding up at the show auction.

I was a pioneer in the Boer goat industry, the first registered stud in North Queensland. Through my work promoting and researching, I was awarded an excellence in business award from the Desert Uplands Regional Development Committee.

On the weekends, when I wasn't doing something goat related, there was always a social gathering of friends or family at our place or at one of theirs. Our veranda was well used for these activities and even doubled as a sleeping quarters for the Hughenden cricket team during their annual three days of cricket "competing" (more like "getting drunk") in the Goldfield Ashes Carnival.

I had volunteered there with my mate Kenny Beare, Johnny's brother, for 20 years. Kenny roped me into it the first year I came home from hospital and it became a tradition from then on. Technically we were volunteers, but the free bar tab more than compensated for the three 16-hour days.

I started work with Dalflin Employment in 1994 as the administration assistant and got promoted to manager after the first year. I had a company car and worked my own hours. I placed jobseekers into jobs all over the town and developed a professional working relationship with many employers and business owners.

With everything I was involved with in my community, I became very well-known and I like to think, well respected. I was recognised for my contributions to my community, not because I had a disability. My friends sometimes even forgot I was in a wheelchair.

This was as close as I was ever going to get to my childhood dream. To the outside world, a perfect dream come true. All the material things were here – but there was still something not quite right.

This is not the way I thought I would feel after finally achieving what I strived for all these years. Sure, there were lots of good times, but there was always an underlying feeling deep down, a sadness of sorts.

Maybe I was expecting too much. I knew eternal happiness would be an unrealistic expectation, but I was nowhere near that.

In fact, I felt the opposite. There was an emptiness about it I couldn't explain.

I started to look for the problem so I could fix it. The only problem was I looked for an external reason, not an internal one.

Something had to change. I thought it might have been my job. I hadn't felt challenged in my work for the last 18 months and had even made a New Year's resolution to find a new career.

The problem was that I wasn't motivated to find a job because I already had one, if that makes sense. There was no pressure.

In the mail one day, Dalflin received the quarterly magazine from "Para Quad," an organisation which supported people with paraplegia and quadriplegia. I never usually opened them; they went straight in the bin. This day I did, just to have a look at the classifieds.

They were advertising a vacant position in their Townsville office for a Peer Support Officer. Must have "lived experience" and a few other general criteria that I could easily meet.

I wrote my application for the job and my resignation letter from my current job and posted them both that same day. After two weeks, I was without a job, but I would have to wait much longer before I heard about my application.

Another fortnight later, a letter arrived inviting me to an interview for the job. With my experience in the employment industry, I never doubted for a minute I would get the job. At the time, I wasn't aware they had headhunted someone else for the position and were merely going through the motions.

I must have interviewed well, because I got the job.

My new job was a 140 km commute each way, an extra three hours a day on top of my eight-hour work day.

The Townsville office serviced a region from Mackay north to the tip and west to the Northern Territory border. My role was to travel the region supporting people with spinal injuries by sharing my lived experiences. It was perfect for me and I was good at it. Driving and talking about something I was a world expert at: me.

Nothing changed for me within, though. Deep down, I knew my job wasn't ever the problem.

I knew what was causing my emptiness, but I didn't have the courage to do anything about it. It was like I didn't want to disappoint everyone. I didn't want to seem like the ungrateful child again.

The problem was, there was no love in my marriage.

I hadn't felt it for many years. I doubt I ever felt true love – more like a strong desire to make a dream come true.

Somehow, Anne and I had gone from telling each other "I love you" every night before we went to sleep to getting into bed in silence. I found myself hoping not to wake her if she went to bed before me or pretending to be asleep if I was first to get into bed.

It's not always the case that a marriage without love has little or no sex, but it was for us. We hadn't been intimate for years. There was no love, and there was no intimacy. Hell, I don't think we even liked each other anymore.

I constantly felt judged, that I wasn't living up to Anne's expectations.

My personality changed when I was in her company. I was the class clown at school and up until then, I thought I could have been a comedian.

"They're laughing because they're embarrassed for you, not because you're funny," she would tell me.

Whenever I acted like myself, I felt like she disapproved and wanted me to be someone else.

I didn't need to hear her tell me; I read her body language and made my own interpretation from my own level of self-worth and self-esteem. Maybe I was reading it all wrong, but you can never be wrong about the way you feel.

Each day I got up at about 4 am, showered, got back into bed to get dressed, and got up. I would make myself a cup of coffee and roll a cigarette for breakfast, and then I would wake Anne to ask her to help me with my shoes before leaving for the day. Since breaking my femur, I couldn't do it myself. I was scared I'd break the other one if I tried.

Every day I left for work before daylight, so I didn't have to feel the judgement. Maybe it wasn't really there, but by this time my imagination had taken it to another level. I was relieved to be in the car, my "safe place."

Ever the optimist, every day I drove home expecting to be met with a smile, like somehow everything had magically changed. I expected to be greeted with that fairy tale, "eyes lighting up" when I came into the room, but it was never there. Instead I saw regret, as if she now regretted her decision to marry me. I doubted if there had ever been a sparkle there.

Anne wasn't stupid; she recognised our marriage was far from healthy and arranged for us to get marriage counselling. To me, this seemed like a setup to point the blame at me. I felt like I was being judged by two people, not just Anne. I believed her motivation was not so much about saving our dying marriage but more about avoiding the embarrassment a failed marriage would cause.

Sadly, I had lost any desire to try to salvage our relationship or our marriage. Instead, I directed my passion into my hobby.

I don't believe our relationship or our marriage was Anne's first priority, either. She directed her attention to her work.

We continued to live in what I considered a toxic relationship.

I don't believe either of us were in denial anymore about the state of our marriage. I consider myself to be the most non-confrontational person – or just plain chicken shit. Either way, I avoided any situation which might lead to discussing our problems.

Anne would leave a copy of *Men Are From Mars, Women Are From Venus* on the shelf beside my toilet, ear marked at the relevant pages. I assumed she wanted me to read it and change accordingly. I never did. I didn't believe I was the one who needed to change.

Instead, I just withdrew into myself even more, hoping it would all go away. I pretty much avoided any serious conversations and stuck to the daily essentials. "What time do I need to pick up the boys from dance?" or "I'll be up the back feeding the goats."

As if to rub salt into my already weeping emotional wound, I returned home from work one night to find Polly dead. She had been my faithful companion for ten years. Whenever I needed comforting, she was always there with those loving eyes of hers.

I really was an emotional wreck. Although I cried myself to sleep that night, I dealt with her loss in a strangely cold way. I think I had gone into some kind of emotional protection shutdown.

We need to stay together for the children, I heard myself saying whenever I started to feel overwhelmed by everything. That's what lots of couples do, and once the kids leave home, they get divorced.

I loved my children and they loved me, too, but what message, what lesson was I teaching them? That it's okay to live a life without the love of your wife or feeling love for her?

I wanted to feel loved unconditionally by my wife, yet I still didn't even love myself unconditionally.

Right from its earliest conception, my dream was the instrument that would make me feel happy.

It was never about the bricks and mortar.

It was never about the farm or the car in the shed or the job or any of that.

It was always about the emotion I would feel once I had it.

I didn't feel it.

Most people would call it a midlife crisis, but I called it coming to the realisation that I was living someone else's dream.

This dream had everything you could ever wish for except one thing. The one thing that makes our dreams, our goals, our visions become a part of us.

The eyes didn't light up.

I was trapped in someone else's dream. I couldn't see a light at the end of the tunnel – only darkness and disappointment.

Each night before I fell asleep, I looked forward to getting into the car in the morning to escape my reality, just for a while.

Yesterday Today Tomorrow

CHAPTER 11
SOULMATES

Just before I was about to jump in the car for my leisurely hour and a half drive home on Friday, 8 July 2005, an email came to me, forwarded on from my old job at Dalflin.

I wonder what that's about? Whatever it is it can wait till Monday.

I didn't give it much thought until I arrived back at work on the Monday morning.

"Hey, do you remember me? Vikki Antaw, we went to school together at Richmond Hill State School."

Vikki (Antaw) Vella was reconnecting with all of her old school friends. She had googled my name and found my old work email address.

Her first day in my grade 6 class came back to me as clear as if it were today.

"How could I forget that long blonde hair and those skinny legs?" I replied. "Yes, of course I remember you."

I had fallen in love with her at first sight. She was my first ever girlfriend. I remembered the birthday parties where the boys all brought a bottle of soft drink and the girls brought a plate to share. We'd play "spin the bottle" or "catch 'n' kiss." She was the one I'd always chase, and I think, looking back, she may not have been running as fast as she could.

I wondered what might have been had her family not left town.

We started to share stories via email about the last 33 years.

We had lived such totally different lives.

Vikki told me how her family moved from town to town and never really settled anywhere. She told me about starting her own family when she was just 18 and how she already had three grandkids.

I told her how I was living the dream, but I'm pretty sure she saw through that façade – not that she said it at the time. Her "bullshit" radar was and still is very accurate, and she doesn't call a spade a shovel.

I gave her the "Facebook" version of my life. I told her all of my good times stories, the funny yarns, the ones that boosted my ego.

Vikki found my storytelling really funny and started sharing my stories with her friends and family.

"He should write a book," they all said. "He's hilarious."

"I will one day," I promised.

For the past ten years I'd been struggling emotionally, but I also had some physical issues I was dealing with. Through overuse I had damaged my elbow and developed a pressure wound. It needed surgery to repair. I'd been on a waiting list for several months and still didn't have a confirmed date for the operation.

One Friday afternoon at about 4 o'clock, I got a call from the PA hospital. "We've had a cancellation. Is there any chance you can be in Brisbane by Tuesday the 12th of September for a surgery on the 15th?"

"You mean next Tuesday?" I was taken by surprise. Knowing how long it takes to get a surgery date and how desperate I was to fix my issue, there was no way I was going to say no. This time, I couldn't leave my response till Monday.

I booked my flights for Sunday before I left work and told Anne the good news as soon as I arrived home that night.

I thought this would be a good opportunity for a face-to-face catch up with Vikki after sharing emails for the last few weeks, so I asked her if she would be able to pick me up from the airport or just catch up for a coffee.

She agreed, but I wasn't prepared for what was about to take place.

We met in the domestic arrivals terminal and greeted each other with the customary "school reunion" hug and then stepped back to do the mandatory "check each other out." Trying to compare this person with the memory of the 30-years-younger one you knew.

My eyes locked onto hers and I couldn't look away. I just stared into her dusty blue eyes for what seemed like an hour. I stared well past that awkward "it's time to look away now" point and on through the "this is getting creepy now" moment.

I don't know why she didn't turn and run for her life, but she just stared right back at me. Maybe she saw the same thing in mine that I saw in hers.

Eventually, one of us said, "How about we have a coffee?" and we did.

At the hospital, so much had changed since the last time I was in the spinal unit. The original ward was long gone. I hardly recognised any of the buildings from back in my day. The culture was still the same.

I had to answer all the questions multiple times.

What's your date of birth?

20 May 1960

How much do you weigh?

God knows, I haven't been on a set of scales in years.

Do you have any allergies?

Don't think so.

Do you drink?

Only when I'm alone or with someone.

Do you smoke?

Yes, about 15 to 20 a day.

The morning of my surgery, a team of doctors came to see me to ask me a bunch of questions they already knew the answers to.

"Do you smoke?"

"Yes."

This one seemed surprised by my answer. "You know if you smoke there's a high chance the surgery won't be successful?"

"Okay. No. I don't smoke." In that moment, I became a non-smoker. I never had another cigarette. That was fortunate, because the new hospital was a NO SMOKING area.

After the successful operation, I stayed another six weeks in hospital to recover and rehabilitate. Those first few weeks confined to bed gave me a lot of time to think about my future, just like they had nearly 30 years earlier.

I came to the decision that I wasn't going to go back to my old life. I wasn't going back to live with Anne. I could still be a father to my children, I just wouldn't be living with them.

Decision made, now I had to find the right way and the right words to tell them. Once I got home, I'd figure all that out.

Out of the blue, Anne called one day to tell me she was flying down for a visit.

"No don't do that," I said. "Don't waste the money on airfares."

"What do you mean?"

"I'm not coming home after I get out of hospital. I'm moving to Townsville."

I just blurted it out. It wasn't what I wanted to say and it certainly wasn't the way I wanted to say it. But that was how it happened; I couldn't take it back or have a do-over. If ever there was a wrong way to break up with Anne, that was it.

She was in total shock. I had blindsided her, and she reacted accordingly. What I had just done to her was despicable, and there was nothing I could do or say to change that.

I could only hope that in time she would find a way to let go of her anger and pick up her pieces.

Typically, in a small town when a couple separates, everybody has to pick a side. Not surprisingly, almost everyone chose Anne's side, and why wouldn't they? I had told no one how I felt. It was my duty as a bloke to keep that shit bottled up inside.

Everyone in town had made their judgement, and most had passed sentence, too. That wasn't a surprise to me, either, but

I was surprised by the judgement I got outside of my circle of friends.

Nursing staff, therapists, and even doctors questioned me about my decision without knowing anything about my situation. My boss and the CEO came to see me after somehow getting word from the grapevine.

I was a little overwhelmed by how quickly I had fallen from grace and the sheer scale of how harshly I was judged and by how many. My immediate reaction was to make judgements back at them.

How dare they stick their noses into my personal affairs! How dare they throw stones from their glass houses! How dare they fabricate lies to support their judgement! Apparently, I'd been having an online affair for months. That was certainly news to both Vikki and me.

My respect for my so-called friends and colleagues would never recover from this.

Vikki had been visiting me in hospital every few days and was just as miffed as I was when I told her.

Up until this point, while I was well aware that there was a connection between us, neither Vikki or I ever spoke of it, let alone acted on it.

That's not how the grapevine saw it, though, and they probably still believe it to this day. While I was upset at the time, I've since discovered that what someone else thinks of you is none of your business, so I just let it go.

Vikki instantly became my only ally, my only friend.

The rumour mill prompted us to start talking about what was going on between us, though.

Vikki was looking for her "ideal partner" and had written a four-page list of essential attributes the successful suitor would possess.

Her sister Pam laughed when she read it and said, "I'm sorry, darling, but God is not available."

I never saw the list, but from what Vikki told me, I didn't tick many of her boxes. Nevertheless, there was an undeniably powerful connection between us, and our relationship quickly moved past the "friend zone."

It's amazing how certain sounds, smells, or tastes can take you back in time to a place or event which holds a special memory. When we kissed for the first time, the taste of her lips immediately took me back to a game of "spin the bottle" in the backyard at Mum's. They tasted just the same as they had in 1971. I was astounded by how vivid my recollection was and how I could recall something so random.

My recovery and rehab progressed nicely and the time came for my first overnight pass.

Vikki's place wasn't super wheelchair accessible, but it was doable.

Anticipating things might get intimate, I had a chat with my good old friend Dr Vernon Hill about "the blue pill." I hadn't ever used it before, but then, it had been ten years. I wanted to make a good impression.

The night didn't quite go as I planned. One of the side-effects of Viagra is it can upset your bowels. It can, and it did that night.

I thought the humiliation of my first three days back at work was the worst thing that could happen, but I was so wrong. Vikki's bathroom was the only part of her house that I couldn't get into. Luckily for me, and the entertainment of her neighbours, she had a plastic stackable chair and a garden hose for me to use to get cleaned up, outside on the back lawn.

Again, to my surprise, Vikki didn't run away from the scary man who'd just shit in her bed. She was in this for the inner me, not the one that everyone else saw.

With the otherwise success of my overnight pass, my discharge date was set for the next week. I suddenly realised I didn't have anywhere to go. I wasn't going home.

I had to find somewhere to live in Townsville, and quickly. A lot had changed since the last time I went house hunting. I'd built my last two homes. I searched realestate.com, but finding a wheelchair accessible rental in Townsville was like trying to find a rocking horse turd.

In desperation, I searched for retirement units, knowing that at least they would have wheelchair access. I found one that was willing to accept a 45-year-old tenant. And so, the prediction of my old rehabilitation team came true: I moved into an old age care facility. Only until I could find something more age appropriate.

Vikki and I had discussed the idea of a long-distance relationship and both agreed that wasn't what we wanted. She decided to sell "Your Office Bitch," the bookkeeping business she had built from scratch, to be with me. She did need to stay a little longer in Brisbane, though, to tie up some loose ends with her business before joining me in Townsville in the new year.

The thought of spending Christmas alone wasn't new to me; I had already done that in my drug and alcohol haze in the '80s. This time was different, though. This would be my first Christmas in ten years where I wouldn't be Santa's helper.

I had never been lonelier and more alone in my life than Christmas Day 2005. I waited in my unit all day for a phone call from Joe or Ben, but it didn't come. I can only assume they didn't ask or their mother didn't prompt them.

While I never second guessed my decision to separate, it was now the reality of this decision really took hold. I felt stranded, friendless, and without a family. I didn't even have my car to go for a drive and escape it all.

Among the disappoint and judgement coming from my family and friends, one man chose to support me. Wayne Brodie called me. "What do you need me to do?" he asked. He was always there whenever I needed a mate and knew I would be there for him.

"Can you pick up my ute and bring it down?"

He arrived with my beloved ute, my .22 rifle, and four cardboard boxes of miscellaneous belongings. The sum of my lifelong accumulated possessions.

The retirement unit couldn't fit much more than that. It wasn't any bigger than a caravan park cabin. A tiny living/kitchen area, even tinier bedroom, and an ensuite. Vikki had truckloads of furniture and belongings. She had inherited her father's nomadic habits to the extent where her kids gave her a replica removal van as a going away gift. We needed somewhere with more room. Much more.

We found a house at Bushland Beach which didn't need much to make it wheelchair friendly. Unlike the renovations Cookie did, this time I used a licensed builder to make the modifications. It had four bedrooms for Vikki's stuff, one of which would become the starting place for her to rebuild her bookkeeping business.

Shortly after, Anne sold up the farm and bought a house in Townsville, so it wasn't long before the boys started to spend some weekends with us.

Somewhere deep down, the "own your own home" candle still flickered. It was all that was left of the raging inferno that was my old dream. God only knew why I was still clinging on to it.

In 2007, Vikki and I bought our first home together. Well, the bank owned it, but we were off the rental roundabout.

One point five acres in Deeragun. We refurbished the existing saddle shed into an office for Vikki's business. Wayne brought me a couple of my favourite goats; he'd rescued them before the farm was sold.

We settled into life on the outskirts of the city. I had my goats and Vikki had her garden. Vikki's business took off and I was now working full time. The boys stayed over every second weekend. Life was good.

I never dreamed a relationship could be like this. Vikki allowed me to be myself. I never felt judged, although when I did or said something she didn't like, she would grin and say through clenched teeth, "I love you." Not being the sharpest tool in the shed, it took me a while to figure out what she was telling me.

We had different tastes and interests in most things, but that's what made it special. Vikki held some very strong spiritual beliefs – not religion, spirituality. We were poles apart in this area, not that I was religious, either. I was more scientific than spiritual.

"If we're here on Earth for a spiritual journey to learn life's lessons," I asked her, "what possible lesson could my baby girls have got?" I knew I could challenge her without her feeling threatened, and I knew she would answer honestly regardless of how I would react.

"Maybe their short lives weren't about their journey," she calmly yet knowingly replied. "Maybe they were here for someone else to learn."

A huge penny dropped for me. Immediately, I recalled the effect they had on so many people. They truly were messengers of love.

Vikki and I shared a very special thing: we loved each other unconditionally.

There was never jealousy. There was never judgement. Even though we didn't always agree with each other, we never argued. We supported each other's decisions, whether we liked them or not. We respected each other's opinions.

As cheesy as it sounds, we truly were soulmates. We were separated once a long time ago, but that would never happen again.

Vikki invested everything into our relationship. She moved 1500 km away from her children and grandchildren to be with me. I knew how much she missed them. I didn't have the same relationship with Joe and Ben. Most times when they were with me, they would rather have been somewhere else.

After four years living in Townsville, our decision to move back to Brisbane wasn't that difficult.

I didn't think the boys would miss having their dad close by. They had a much closer relationship with their mother. In comparison to the Mackereths, the extended Franzmann clan was much more family orientated.

There's a general consensus about always putting family above everything else. Strangely, I don't share that belief. I felt bad admitting feeling that way, but that's just how it is. Sure, I'd love to see them more often but I know they're happy where they are, and there's always Facebook.

Not really wanting to give up our country lifestyle, we found a rental property in Fernvale at the bottom of the Brisbane Valley.

There was a great country pub close enough for us to walk to and the township had a real friendly spiritual feel about it.

This was the place. We felt that we were home.

Yesterday Today Tomorrow

CHAPTER 12

SHARING THE LIVED EXPERIENCE

Before we left Townsville, I had submitted a business proposal to my boss outlining the benefits of restructuring the peer support program. She agreed, and my position was relocated to Brisbane, where I would work in the spinal unit at the PA Hospital, supporting the newly injured patients and their families.

I loved my new job and the 60 km commute to and from work each day.

By this time, I had plenty of experience to share, almost 35 years of living with a spinal cord injury. I wanted to share my lived experience with newly injured patients in the spinal unit. I knew from my own time there how easy it was to think there was no future. I never could have dreamed, way back then, lying in traction in my Edgerton bed, that I would achieve any of the incredible things I had.

So much had changed for me, yet there were only some minor changes at the hospital, it seemed. The whole hospital campus was a no smoking area. I already knew that much, but there was one other thing missing. There were no Edgerton beds. No more turning patients every two or four hours, and they used hoists instead of the old "top and tail" manual lifting.

Advances in surgical techniques meant that most patients now had their fractures stabilised with metal plates. They didn't spend weeks in traction or wrapped in fibreglass casts. A great step forward for their physical recovery, but they no longer had the opportunity I did to adjust emotionally to their new circumstances.

Instead, they went from a normal, active life one day to being plonked unceremoniously into a wheelchair the next with all the added extras that come with it.

"The poor bastards," I thought. I couldn't comprehend how much they must be going through in their minds. All the pictures in their minds erased and nothing to replace them. There didn't seem to be any extra support put in place to compensate emotionally for the new "fast tracked" physical process.

Now the need for psychological support was even greater than in my day. The peer support program was and still is a vital part of their rehabilitation journey.

There were three of us in the team, with a combined lived experience of 75 years to share.

We were responsible for giving the patients and their families hope for the future. Not hope for physical recovery. Hope for recreating a vision for a full and successful life after spinal cord injury.

Our job was to inspire them through sharing how we had achieved our own visions, how we had overcome barriers, and how we continued to set ourselves bigger and better challenges with or without a spinal injury.

This challenge inspired me and gave me a new passion for my future. I could see myself loving my new role.

It answered my father's question: "What on earth possessed you to dive into the fucking Fletcher?"

I was supposed to.

One of my co-workers, Katie Franz, was quite new to the peer support role. Although new, she had a gift for connecting with patients. She brought with her a vast collection of her own lived experience and a perspective that only a woman can give.

We struck up an immediate bond. It was more than a bond. Katie filled a void in my personal life. One that had been left by my beautiful baby girls, Kate and Veronica.

Katie had recently lost her dad in tragic circumstances, and I believe it was no coincidence our paths crossed at this time. There was a love between us, a love that has since grown to include our partners.

We evolved into a great professional partnership and used our personal connection to take our work to another level.

"How was your drive to work this morning?" Katie would ask, making sure she could be overheard by the patients.

"I had a great run today, only 35 minutes." I knew straightaway what she was doing.

"How can you drive a car?" One of the patients' curiosity always got the better of them.

This would lead into a long conversation about vehicle modifications, transferring into a car, getting a wheelchair in, and everything else they needed to know about driving.

I'd ask Katie about how her kids were doing at school.

"Did you have children before your accident?" the female patients would ask.

"No. All three of them after," she would explain.

"So, you were married before your accident, then?"

"No. I was only 16. I met my first husband a couple of years after I got out of hospital."

"Oh."

Seeing the cogs of the patients' brains ticking over as they processed the information always made me feel warm inside. Knowing that we were helping them to paint themselves new pictures gave me the best job satisfaction. I would have done it for free if I hadn't had rent to pay.

Always looking for ways to improve our services, Spinal Life Australia (formally Para Quad) found a new program specifically developed by the Canadian Spinal Injuries Association and the Pacific Institute, "Discovering the Power in Me" (DPM). DPM helps people discover their power to find their inner strength, think effectively, and recreate a positive future for themselves.

The whole team travelled to Sydney to participate in the three-day DPM workshop. We then received another two days of training to be qualified to deliver the workshop to others.

It was a life-changing experience for me and I couldn't wait to share my newly acquired knowledge with patients in the spinal unit. Unfortunately, the senior staff there didn't share my enthusiasm and wouldn't allow us to present it in the hospital. I couldn't understand their logic, but we had to abide by their rules.

Over the next four years, we ran the DPM workshops for people after they had been discharged from hospital and for others living with spinal injury in the community.

Seeing a group of people all having simultaneous lightbulb moments gave me such a buzz. I would be on a high for days after every workshop and just wanted to share it with the world.

All the modules made sense to me. They were like a simple English version of complex psychological techniques. I realised that I had been using most of them already but just didn't know what they were called.

DPM added another dimension to my passion to help people by sharing my lived experience and my newfound knowledge.

Not long after Vikki and I moved to Fernvale in September 2010, it started to rain. It continued for weeks and weeks with only a few fine days until Christmas. The rain intensified to flood proportions. The 2011 floods were devastating, and we were right in the mix of it. All the houses across the street from us went under water. Luckily, ours didn't. It came to within a few inches of coming into our house, not that we stayed to watch. We moved back in the next day, isolated by flood waters and without power for a week.

It was amazing to watch our community come together to help each other, yet heart-wrenching to watch those who had lost everything wander aimlessly.

They couldn't see a future any more. Theirs just got washed away. They desperately needed help – help I knew I could give them.

I knew the DPM workshops could give them back a future. With permission from work, I approached the Somerset Regional Council to offer some workshops to help those who had lost so much.

With Katie and Vikki's help, we ran four workshops. I was blown away at how they were received and realised these techniques could help anyone, not just those who had experienced physical trauma. A seed was planted in me. Maybe I could spread the word to an even wider audience.

Spinal Life experienced a number of CEO changes and major restructures during the same four-year period. One of the reforms involved the decision to stop running the DPM workshops.

I felt like I was in the lead on lap 18 at Bathurst and someone rolled a rock onto the track. We had just lost one of the most powerful tools we had. This decision really affected me.

I'd been working with this organisation for ten years, and I started to think maybe we weren't on the same page any more.

I took the opportunity to take my long service leave and process where I was and what my future role might look like.

We decided to try the "grey nomad" lifestyle for a while. I designed a wheelchair accessible caravan and had it custom built. The build went months over schedule and we finally took delivery the day before our rental lease expired.

Without the luxury of a test run, we hooked up the caravan and headed off on our adventure. Adventure is so far from the right word to describe it. Trauma, living nightmare, fucking hell on wheels. All much more accurate descriptions. I'm not going to relive it in detail now. One hundred and twenty-eight days after leaving we returned, never to set foot in another caravan again.

We reached our lowest point in our relationship with a face-to-face swearing match on the Main Street of Echuca before finally succumbing to the stress and returning home. Just to add salt to our wounds, the exhaust pipe fell off the car on the last leg home, and then the van fell off its legs in the van park. Seeing the person you love in the foetal position rocking and sobbing uncontrollably is something I never want to see again.

After a brief stay in a granny flat, we found a place in Karalee. We needed to put down roots for a while. A good while.

Even though Vikki and I knew we were soulmates and would always be together, we made the decision to get married. Third time lucky for both of us. We both knew we weren't going to need luck with what we felt for each other.

Having sorted out our living arrangements and our marital status, we turned our attention back to our careers.

With a little prompting from me, Vikki decided to give up her bookkeeping work to concentrate on her life's true vocation, spiritual healing. She set up her healing room in a spare bedroom and business boomed for her.

I went back to work at Spinal Life. Instead of resuming my role as team leader, I preferred the more hands-on, face-to-face peer support with the patients. Business plans, budgets, and quality assurance never floated my boat.

Something in me wanted to share my lived experience with a wider audience. Without the pressure of being the leader, I was able to cut back my hours with Spinal Life and give myself time to branch out. I enrolled in a Diploma of Life Coaching. These new skills would enhance my ability to do my current job but also open up other opportunities. It was never my intention to become a life coach and coach individuals on a one-to-one basis. I wanted to add another aspect to my skill set by adding a formal qualification.

I'd always held a desire to get on the public speaking circuit. Through my work with Spinal Life, I'd had a few speaking engagements already which were very well received.

Armed with my life experience, the DPM modules, and a diploma, I believed I had what it took to become a professional motivational speaker.

A good friend had started a website called CrowdPleaser. Basically, it connected entertainers with gigs and received a small commission. I uploaded my profile and waited for the job offers to come flooding in. I quickly learned that there are a lot of motivational speakers out there. To be successful, I needed to stand out. I needed a point of difference.

Oh, and marketing. I'm shit at marketing. Great speaker, shit at marketing.

Being different, being unique, would get me so far. Getting a professional marketing person would get me further, but I knew the most important part about speaking or any communication was establishing a connection with the audience. Something I had in common with them.

My commonality is change.

Everyone wants to know about change. How to cope with it. How to create it.

I'd been doing it all my life.

CHAPTER 13

AGENTS OF CHANGE

Over the course of my life, I have experienced some life-changing events from both external and internal forces. I have learned how to adapt to change and, more importantly, how to create my own change.

Most people would say that having a spinal injury when I was only 18 would be the experience or event that has had the most profound effect on me and my future. Yes, it certainly was traumatic and profoundly affected me in a physical sense, but it didn't really contribute much to my development emotionally or spiritually, not in the long term at least. Nor did it change the way I think.

People might also say that the death of my two children within weeks of each other would've been one of the most traumatic, and yes, it was. I think of them almost every day, but they are trapped in the past and no one will ever know what might've been had they survived.

Their death has had a huge impact on my journey to date, and I will carry the strength they gave me into my future, but their short lives have still not affected me in what I believe to be the most profound way.

I can't say I can identify a life-changing moment; however, there are three people who have made the most profound effect on my life.

I consider them to be my agents of change.

The first was a man I'd never even met, yet he created the most significant change – not only to my life in the present but also to my future. If ever I were forced to find something in life I regret (I have none), it would be that I never got to meet Lou Tice in person before he passed.

Lou and his wife Dianne founded the Pacific Institute (TPI) as "a corporation dedicated to human fulfillment" in 1971, and their work still lives on to this day. They created "Discovering the Power in Me."

My life changed as a result of attending his workshop. It unlocked my power to create meaningful and sustainable change simply by changing the way I think. Every day I listen to Lou's words in my mind: "Your current thoughts determine your future."

I was privileged to be trained by TPI to facilitate "Discovering the Power in Me" and have since delivered it to dozens of participants. I trust that I too have had an influence on some of them in the same way Lou has had on me.

Sadly, this program is no longer offered by TPI, but I continue to live by, and share, the wisdom of its principles in my own way. I hope that Lou's work will live on with me.

The second agent of change was Sue Henry, whom I'd met only once and very briefly. She taught me the power of forgiveness. Sue's story is incredible and challenged me to rethink the way I treat others and myself.

Sue discovered her own power of forgiveness several months after her elderly father died as a result of a serious assault in his home. She has since developed an app, "I forgive you," to help others to let go of their anger and find their own inner peace.

Through my short conversation with Sue, I realised that holding on to anger is like drinking poison and expecting the other person to die. She taught me how to become stronger by replacing anger and resentment with forgiveness and empathy.

I have forgiven all of my judges. I have let go of the past, not the actual events, but the way I think about the events. I no longer allow past negative emotions to set my mood.

I now know how anger, revenge, resentment, regrets, and all those negative emotions simply hijack my thoughts and steer me towards a place I don't want to be.

It's perfectly normal for those emotions to come into my mind, but it's not okay for them to stay there. It's a bit like when relatives come to visit: it's good when they leave.

Every day I am thankful for meeting her, and every day I use the power of forgiveness to grow stronger.

The third agent of change is my beautiful wife. Vikki Mackereth not only loves me unconditionally but has also taught me how to love unconditionally. Everyone has heard the old cliché: "You have to learn to love yourself before you can love someone else. Because it's only when we love ourselves that we feel worthy of someone else's love."

Unconditional love is the most incredible gift I can give anyone. I now give it freely to myself and those who are close to me.

Before reconnecting with Vikki, I didn't understand what it meant.

Loving myself unconditionally means that I can be myself without caring what anyone else thinks of me.

It means I can love the way I look without caring about my body image. I used to go to great lengths to hide my hands so people wouldn't know I couldn't use them. I loathed my "quad pod" to the point where I never allowed anyone to see it. I never made love with the lights on. Since I learned how to love myself unconditionally, I can go outside without a shirt and enjoy the sun's glorious rays on my bare skin.

Now, in the midst of middle age spread, my tummy is even bigger. Even more to love.

This is truly the most liberating of changes that I have experienced in my life.

I am my own best agent of change.

My outlook on life enables me to engage in the emotion and detail of every moment as it's happening and to experience it for what it is, whether positive or negative.

It's my belief we were meant to experience a balance of both.

Success and failure.

Happiness and sorrow.

Pleasure and pain.

Without the one, how can we truly experience the other?

Living in this very moment, I have discovered how to get the best out of my life's experiences.

I cherish my past and draw strength from it.

I visualise my future to give me something to strive for.

My life is a work in progress, and it's all happening right now.

I know what I need to do to create my future, to adapt to and create my own change.

Benjamin Franklin said, "in this world, nothing is certain except death and taxes." I would argue there's at least one more.

Change.

There are around eight billion people in the world, and yet no two of us are exactly the same. We do all share one thing in common, though, and that is that our lives will all be subject to change.

How we cope with or create that change will determine how successful we are in life.

Change comes in two types.

The change that happens from external forces and the change that comes from within.

The first type of change isn't as common as we'd like to think. Natural disasters like fire, floods, and cyclones are examples of external forces which cause change, and that's about it.

Accidents, injury, or illness cause change, too, but I would argue that we still play a contributing factor in this change simply by the choices we make.

Mostly, this externally generated change is out of our control. We can really only control the way we allow it to affect us.

Nearly 100 percent of the change which affects us on any given day comes from within. We generate it ourselves, or at the very least, we play a contributing role in it.

This change can be positive, moving us towards our desired state, or it can be negative, moving us away from where we want to be.

Either way, we still created it.

Why would we consciously create negative change for ourselves? Mostly we don't.

We only control about 10 percent of our internal change with conscious thought. The rest is generated automatically by our subconscious thoughts and accumulated memories. It's like we're on autopilot or cruise control.

This gives us the illusion it's created from external forces. The good news is, we can reset the cruise control.

I have learned how to reset my own cruise control, how to create positive change and create my own successful future.

I have identified what I believe to be the eight keys to meaningful and sustainable change.

Someone smarter than me will probably tell you that these are all well-documented psychological theories, and that's most likely true.

However, I haven't learned them through studying philosophy or psychology at university. I've accumulated them through my life experiences, through not only spinal cord injury but also everyday life.

Each of these keys have transformed my life and are applicable to anyone in any walk of life; however, they are most applicable when dealing with trauma and overcoming significant diversity.

PART TWO

THE 8 KEYS

Yesterday Today Tomorrow

8 KEYS TO MEANINGFUL & SUSTAINABLE CHANGE

1. IDENTITY
You cannot do something you are not.

2. THOUGHT POWER
You act and behave in accordance with your subconscious thoughts.

3. VISUALISATION
All meaningful and sustainable change starts on the inside and works its way out.

4. BELIEF
Everything is possible unless you believe otherwise.

5. SELF WORTH
You will never receive or achieve anything you don't feel worthy of.

6. COMFORT ZONES
The place that comforts you is the place that imprisons you.

7. SELF-TALK
You can talk yourself into doing anything you want to – anything at all.

8. OWNERSHIP
Nothing (and no one) can make you change unless you choose to change.

Yesterday Today Tomorrow

CHAPTER 14
IDENTITY

As human beings, we are all individuals, and we all have our own unique identities and personalities. It's what makes us who we are. Everybody knows this, but what everybody doesn't know is how much of an effect our identity has on what we can and cannot do. How our personality affects our performance, if you like.

Most of us haven't really given it much thought. We just are who we are. We don't realise that our actions are completely controlled by our identity and our core personal values.

Our core personal values are mostly in control of our conscious thoughts and actions. They're the rules by which we choose to live our lives.

Our identity, on the other hand, influences our subconscious thoughts; once established, we subconsciously become a slave to our identity.

One thing I've learned about myself is that my actions are always loyal to my identity. I don't do anything which doesn't fit in with who I am. It's normal for me. It's what I do, and no matter how hard I consciously try to change what I do, it never seems to work.

Do you know you're not born with your identity? No.

I wasn't born with a cigarette in my mouth. I took on the identity of being a smoker – it was the cool thing to do in the '70s.

Every single aspect of our identity, we have created (or someone else has created and we've accepted it). It doesn't matter whether we put it in there or someone else does; once it's there, that's how you act.

So, when I say "change your identity and your behaviour will follow suit," what is the key word in that sentence?

YOUR!

Your identity. It's your identity: you own it, you created it, and you can change it.

First, though, you have to know who you are now. What are normal behaviours for you and what are not? This is the first step to understanding why you act the way you do rather than the way you *want to*.

Our identities are very complex and have many aspects to them, but the one thing we all have in common is that once our identity is established, we act in accordance with that identity.

Every action we take is subject to our subconscious identity. Our behaviour must match our identity, otherwise we won't be able to sustain it.

Another word for our actions and behaviours is our habits. No matter how hard you try CONSCIOUSLY to change your habits, you usually find you go back to being true to your identity.

Your brain is hardwired to make sure that your actions and behaviours match your identity. SUBCONSCIOUSLY.

I started to create my own identity the day I was born. We all did. Even though I have no recollection of anything earlier than when I was about 5 years old, I was storing information away in my subconscious mind, my memory, that would mould me as the person I am today.

Your identity is a DIY project. We are all a creation of our own accumulated thoughts.

It's also a work in progress, like a city.

Most cities start out with the erection of a few tents, then buildings, roads, and businesses. Cities are constantly expanding. Our identities have developed in a similar way, and they too continue to grow and change.

Some parts of cities are knocked down to make room for newer, more modern buildings, while others are National Trust Heritage-listed and will never change.

We change, too, like the way we follow the latest fashion or interest.

Everything we experience in life, we consciously process and analyse. We think about how we came to the experience, the choices we made, what happened, and the consequences.

Most importantly, we store in our memory how we felt about it: the emotion.

It's this emotion we lock into our subconscious mind, never to be forgotten. Sure, in time, we lose a lot of the details of each experience from our conscious memory, but the emotion is never lost.

The next time any of our five senses pick up something the same or similar, subconsciously we recall the emotion and act to either move towards or away from the experience, depending on whether it was a positive or a negative one.

When I was a kid, I hated the taste of pumpkin to the point where I would dry retch. At dinner time, I wasn't allowed to leave the table until I had eaten everything on my plate. The nights we had pumpkin, which was most nights, I was traumatised. I tried everything to avoid eating it. Every night, it was the last thing left on my plate and the last taste left in my mouth. I don't eat pumpkin now. Just the thought of it sends shivers up my spine.

That's heritage listed; it's not likely to change.

Most of us have parts of our identity which seem permanently fixed. Our habits. Most of us have habits that we are trying to break, like smoking.

I had my first cigarette when I was 11 years old. Mum would make me chaperone my sister when she met her boyfriend at the Apex park just down the road from our house. She couldn't have made a better choice; I was an annoying little shit towards my big sister most of the time.

Dave would pull the pack of Marlboro out of his sleeve and offer me one. He thought that would keep me out of their hair for a while.

I'd take it, run away and pigeon puff it, and then be back again before they had a chance to get too cosy.

He'd give me another one to get rid of me. "Here, now piss off and leave us alone."

You couldn't really say I was a smoker then, but once I started buying my own, Viscount 5-pack every Saturday night at the Regent cinema, I had taken on the identity.

I was a smoker! For the next 30 years I did what all smokers do: I smoked.

Identity

If ever I needed to fill out paperwork, insurance policies or the like, I'd tick the smoker box. Are you a smoker? Yes! I was constantly reaffirming my identity, setting it in concrete in my subconscious.

Like most smokers, it wasn't long before I started trying to quit, and for most of my smoking life, I was a smoker trying to quit doing what smokers do: smoke cigarettes.

And there's the problem.

Once something becomes part of your identity, part of who you are, you can't change it, at least not easily. I tried nicotine patches, hypnotherapy... You name it, I tried it. Nothing worked for more than a few hours.

I don't smoke now. I'm not a smoker anymore. My actions match my identity.

I learned that if I want to change "what I do," I must first change "who I am."

I became a non-smoker in my mind. I declared myself to be a non-smoker. I said it out loud: "I'm not a smoker." And I never had another cigarette.

I made a vow. I believed it, and it got locked away in my subconscious as part of my identity.

Just like the city, many people have contributed to the construction of my identity.

Over the years I've been judged and labelled.

"He's the class clown," my teacher would announce to the class. I liked that label; I felt important and I got attention, so I accepted it. My behaviour matched my title.

Years later, my cricket coach said the words to me infamously credited to Shane Warne: "Can't bowl, can't throw." I believed him. He was the coach; he would know. I applied the same skill level to my batting and catching.

Often when a label is given to you by someone of authority, you just accept it. You don't even know you have the option to reject it.

Most of my sporting coaches made similar statements about my abilities. They too got locked away as part of my identity, and my performances matched my identity. Who knows what I might have achieved if I hadn't accepted their labels?

If I hadn't discarded those labels later in life, maybe I wouldn't have won four gold medals for my country.

Had I accepted my doctors' and therapists' label – *you'll never be able to live independently* – maybe my wheelchair would define me and not my achievements.

It doesn't matter if you created your identity or if someone else labelled you.

The way you change your identity is by changing the way you think.

The first step is to get to know your identity better. Think about the labels that we put on ourselves, or those that others have put on us.

Look at the typical behaviours (habits) associated with each label. Look at what's not typical behaviour for each.

If you identify with a particular label and the change you desire is about non-typical behaviours, you've got a problem. You won't be able to do it, or you won't be able to sustain it.

YOU MUST CHANGE YOUR IDENTITY FIRST!

CHAPTER 15
THOUGHT POWER

Apart from our basic bodily functions, everything we do starts as a thought before it becomes an action.

We don't move our muscles without first thinking about moving them. That's why our thoughts are so powerful – they control everything we do. That's why it's so important to take control of our thoughts, because otherwise they take control of us.

We need to understand the basics of how our brains and our thoughts work.

I like to think about the brain as a factory with all of its different departments. You've got your reptile brain (WH&S Department). There's a part called the reticular activating system (RAS), which is like the loading dock where the raw product is delivered. There are specialist departments for your senses, processing departments (where the thinking goes on), warehouses (where your memories are stored). It's a huge factory. There are departments for your emotions, your motor skills, your bodily functions... The list is endless.

I like to think about the mind as the business systems. This is more about how your thought processes work. (QA people would be getting excited about this bit, yeah?) You have your conscious thought processes: perception, association, evaluation, and decision-making. Your subconscious (memory) stores your identity, truth, habits, and attitudes, but it also does so much more. It also maintains sanity. It creates drive and energy. It resolves conflict. Maybe it's HR.

Arguably, the most important part of any business/factory is management. The managers tell everyone what to do. In the context of your mind, think of it as your conscience, your ego, or your self-talk. Those conversations you have with yourself all day, the conversations you're having with yourself right now as you're processing what you're reading.

The best bit about this factory though, is that YOU ARE THE CEO.

Ultimately, the buck stops with you. If part of your mind, one of your managers, isn't serving you well, you can just sack them. Actually, these days you would be required to try to re-train them first.

And that's exactly what you need to do.

It's such a complex topic: your brain, your mind, your thoughts, your emotions, your memories, your self-talk, how they all work together and depend on each other. It would take a million books to cover every aspect, so I'm going to just talk about some of the processes that are crucial to our ability to make meaningful and sustainable change.

Albert Einstein once said, "If you can't explain it simply, you don't understand it well enough." So, when it comes to change, here's my simple version of what you need to know about your brain and your mind.

Here's the first thing you need to understand:

As we go about our daily activities, a lot of our decision-making happens automatically. It's subconscious. It's like we're on autopilot. Your reptile brain is on autopilot to keep you safe.

When something threatening happens, i.e. a wild animal attacks you, your reptile brain automatically kicks in to make you fight, flee, or freeze. If you touch a hot stove, reptile brain instinctively makes you retract your hand. It may also cause an expletive to automatically fly out of your mouth.

Mother Nature and evolution programmed your reptile brain. You can't really change that.

It's a fear-based process which works on the basis of something bad happening if you don't do something about it immediately. This reptilian survival instinct is embedded in us, so it's almost impossible to change. The closest we can come is by gaining some control over our fears.

Gaining control over your fear is another very complex topic just on its own, and I'm not going to cover in much detail. But I can share my two little gems about fear.

Fear is future focused. You're not afraid of the snake. You're actually afraid of being bitten by the snake. Your fear is based on an event that hasn't happened yet.

Bring your fear into the present. Have I been bitten yet? Am I likely to be fatally bitten by this rubber snake? Do I really need to be afraid of my present situation?

You know how crazy you look when you nearly step on a snake and you're jumping around all over the place or you walk through a spider's web? Reptile brain doesn't care about your sanity; its only job is to keep you safe.

Reptile brain believes safety is more important than sanity.

It won't let you go out of your comfort zone, either, just in case you get hurt. You might want to step outside to grow or change, but reptile brain is very clever and will usually come up with a way to keep you safe. Consciously, you don't even know it's happening. That's the problem; that's how clever the subconscious is.

There is a way to get yourself out of your comfort zones. though, and we'll talk more about how to do that in Chapter 19.

Okay. Here's the second thing you need to understand:

We're constantly being bombarded with information from our senses. What we see, what we hear, what we touch, taste, and smell. All this information gets converted into thoughts. It's estimated the average person has around 70,000 thoughts a day. Too much information, too many thoughts for our tiny little brains to process. Our RAS acts as a filter to help us cope with this information overload.

It only lets in information that is relevant to us. So, we're actually getting a censored version of the truth outside, a little bit like commercial media.

Our RAS is on autopilot, too. It's also working subconsciously, but Mother Nature didn't do its programming.

Who programmed the RAS? We did, in much the same way we created our identities. We're continuing to install the updates with every choice we make, every consequence, every experience, every emotion.

We started programming it at birth. We installed updates as we developed our personalities, our memories, our beliefs, and our core personal values. So, as the RAS filters the information which is getting into our brain and interpreting it based on our own programming, we're not seeing what is actually going on. We're seeing what will support our pre-programming. When I say seeing, I mean see, hear, smell, touch, and taste.

We only see the bits we want to see. So, when I looked at a cigarette packet, I didn't see the health warning or the horrific image, I only saw the brand name and the quantity of the pack. That's why that campaign failed.

It's called a scotoma. The biggest danger with scotomas is that once you "lock on" to something, you "lock out" everything else.

Scotomas can be temporary, too.

Ever lost your keys?

Yeah, and you're searching everywhere for them. In your head, you're telling yourself you can't find your keys. Someone says, "what are you doing?" and you say, "I've lost my keys. I can't find them."

They walk into the room, pick them up off the coffee table (where you've already looked), and hand them to you – and you're all like, "but I looked there and they weren't there, you had them in your pocket, didn't you?"

No. You didn't see them because you kept telling yourself you couldn't find them; your brain just reinforced your belief by building a scotoma to seeing the keys. You see your brain, as complex as it is, can't cope with two conflicting beliefs at the one time.

So, while you're telling yourself you can't find the keys, what would make you look crazy is actually seeing the keys.

The RAS part of your brain believes it's more important to be sane than successful.

There's another part to this principle, too. It's called the self-fulfilling prophecy. You know how this one works. You wake up in the morning and tell yourself how your day is going to go.

Sometimes you say to yourself, "It's going to be a shitty day today, I just know it." And what happens? Shitty stuff happens. Because you're always right, yeah? You know what, though? Good stuff happens, too, but your RAS filters it out because you programmed it to look for the shitty stuff.

Whenever I'm running late for work, I seem to get every red light. There are 21 sets of traffic lights between my house and where I work. I've counted them. The most red lights I've ever got is eight. When I'm in a rush, I notice the red lights more than the green ones. I'm looking for them; my RAS is filtering out the green. Each red light confirms my initial thought that I'm going to be late for work.

Once again, this is going on subconsciously; we don't even know it's happening.

WE THINK WE SEE THE TRUTH.

The next thing, and in my opinion the most important one of all:

Before, when I talked about the managers in your brain factory, your conscience, your ego, the self-talk that goes on... You've probably noticed that sometimes it's like a conversation going on in there, a debate or even an argument.

You know how sometimes you say something to yourself like, "I'm not watching The Bachelor tonight, I've got too much to do on my book." Almost immediately my other self says sarcastically, "Yeah, right, like that's going to happen. You know we're down to the last two roses."

These conversations are critical to how our brains get programmed. Your self-talk is the most valuable tool you have, to control not only your conscious thoughts but also your subconscious thought processes.

YOU MUST USE YOUR SELF-TALK TO CONTROL YOUR THOUGHTS OR YOUR THOUGHTS WILL CONTROL YOU!

There's an old Cherokee Indian story you may have heard before, about two wolves.

An old Cherokee is teaching his grandson about life. *A fight is going on inside me*, he tells the boy.

It is a terrible fight and it is between two wolves. One is evil – he is anger, envy, sorrow, regret, greed, arrogance, self-pity, guilt, resentment, inferiority, lies, false pride, superiority, and ego.

He continues, *the other is good – he is joy, peace, love, hope, serenity, humility, kindness, benevolence, empathy, generosity, truth, compassion, and faith. The same fight is going on inside you – and inside every other person, too.*

The grandson thought about it for a minute and then asked his grandfather, *Which wolf will win?*

The old Cherokee simply replied, *the one you feed.*

Finally, I want to talk about goals:

Because we, as human beings, are goal focused (or teleological, if you want to use the big words), we must always have a goal or goals. Not just to be moving forwards, but to live and survive.

Another word for a goal is an intention, and they come in all shapes and sizes.

Some are complex and detailed: I intend to build my dream home.

Some are very basic: I'm going to the toilet.

Some are long term: one day I'm going to retire to the Gold Coast.

Some are short term: I'm going to mow the lawn now.

Some of them are one-offs: I'm going to get my diploma.

Some are continually repeated: I'm going to catch the bus to work.

Some we write down on paper or put on a vision board, but most we just store in our brain.

The common thing about our goals is that they are always visionary. They are always about a future event or state of being.

We always create the goal first and then go about taking the steps towards achieving them.

The two most important things about a goal are the detail (what will it look like) and the belief (I can do it). You don't even have to know how you're going to achieve it. If you give yourself a vivid picture and believe in it, your subconscious brain will show you how. It's a genius.

The critical thing about goals, though, is that you must give yourself NEW goals or your brain will just default back to the old ones.

My book writing goal: "I'm not going to watch TV tonight."

Okay, so what am I going to do?

That's why New Year's resolutions don't work; we don't give ourselves replacement goals.

Subconscious brain isn't waiting around for you to come up with the new goal. It's already getting creative trying to achieve your old goal of "watching *The Bachelor*."

Once I discovered the power of my thoughts, my life has been a process of continuous improvement, learning how to control my thoughts and use them to move me towards where I want to be.

I realised my subconscious thoughts control 90 percent of what I do and it's on autopilot.

I now know that even though my conscious mind only controls 10 percent of my behaviour, it's enough to reprogram my autopilot.

Sure, it's a work in progress, but that's the exciting part.

Understanding how it works is the first step towards making it work better.

CHAPTER 16
VISUALISATION

Human beings are teleological. We're goal-oriented and need goals to survive. We've already touched a little bit on the sort of goals we have in our everyday life. Short term, long term, complex, simple, the goals that keep us alive, the goals that take us in the direction we want to go.

That might make you think that without giving yourselves a conscious goal you would wander aimlessly with no direction or even die. That's not quite true. Our brains need to have a goal, or a business plan, if you like; if you don't give it a new one, it simply subconsciously refers back to the old one – the default goal or the last goal.

It doesn't matter; it just has to have a goal. New goal, old goal, it's all the same to your subconscious brain.

Your job is to give yourself a new goal and make it more dominant than the old goal; remember the two wolves.

You've got to set the intention, or your subconscious brain will set it for you.

You've got to think about what you do want, not what you don't want.

Research has found that 90 percent of the thoughts we have today are the same as the thoughts we had yesterday. So, if you don't change your thoughts, tomorrow will look pretty much the same as today. And the next day and the next day and so on.

You must involve all of your senses to "visualise" your goals, not just sight, to make it more vivid in your mind than your old goals.

What does it look like? Give yourself a detailed image in colour if you can – a 3D image or, even better, a moving image, a video.

Who else is there? Where is it?

What does it sound like? A video with sound effects.

What does it feel, smell, and taste like? Smell vision.

What emotions does it invoke in you? The more vividly you imagine the new, the more dissatisfied you become with the old. This creates your drive, your desire to feel the emotion.

Here's the trick about goals: your goals not only must be vivid and invoke emotion, but also must be ABOUT THE FUTURE, BUT IN THE PRESENT TENSE. By that I mean you must visualise them and think about them as if they have already been achieved.

Visualisation

That's what elite athletes and successful people do. They identify with the result, not the race. In their minds they've already won, and then their performance matches their belief.

Why is that important? While you're consciously thinking about your goals as already being achieved, the messages coming into your subconscious are telling it that they haven't been achieved.

OMG! It's going into meltdown.

You know how it is about sanity; it's got to get creative and make your outside reality match your inside thoughts. It's called the cognitive dissonance theory; it's got to have order. It can't cope with conflict.

So, all of a sudden, you start to get new ideas. Ideas that will help you achieve your goal. You start to see things that were previously blocked by a scotoma.

You need to feel the emotion associated with that achievement, too; it's very important. You see, our stored memories are more about the emotion we felt, not so much the experience itself. Every time you think of a memory, you relive the event, but you also relive the emotion that came with that event. You reinforce your beliefs from that experience and you reaffirm who you've become because of it. Your identity.

Fulfilling our goals is all about the emotion we experience, not the goal. When you finally get the promotion at work you've been trying for. It's not the duties of that job you're after; it's the feeling you get while you're doing them.

You might think your goal is to own a new BMW convertible. No. Your goal is the feeling you have when you're driving your new BMW convertible or even just washing it on a Sunday afternoon.

We set goals for everything we do: small things like choosing what clothes we're going to wear. We aren't choosing them just to cover ourselves; that's not the goal. We're choosing them to make us feel a particular way. The emotion is the goal. It's always the emotion.

The visions you give yourself and the emotions that you feel are triggered by the words you use when you talk to yourself. The words you use are the key. You must tell yourself the right things.

WORDS ▶ PICTURES ▶ EMOTIONS

There's a second part to visualisation, too. A formula that I learned from Lou Tice about the way our beliefs are formed. Our reality, our truth if you like, or more accurately, what we are telling ourselves is the truth.

IMAGINATION × VIVIDNESS = REALITY (I×V=R)

Your new (yet to be achieved) reality and your existing (stored in memory) reality are both created in the same way.

Imagination, the thoughts we have about an event (past, present, or future), and the self-talk we are using to describe that event.

Vividness. By vividness, I mean when we get a clear picture with emotion, and the picture and emotion are repeated.

Reality. This then becomes our reality. Not the real reality, but the reality that we create in our subconscious memory. The reality that programs our RAS and, to some degree, our reptile brain. This created reality is also responsible for our identity.

You know how some memories are more vivid than others? It's all about how often we think about them and how often we experience that emotion – good emotions and bad emotions.

That's the key to creating the reality you need for your meaningful and sustainable change. Repetition.

The more you increase imagination and vividness, the sooner it becomes reality.

Visualisation

The law of attraction suggests that you draw to yourself that which you think about. That's true, but you have to do it more than once. If that were the case, everyone would have everything they ever thought about. No. You have to do it over and over and over and over and over. And over and over and over.

The best way to make your new goals stronger than your old goals, your new reality more vivid than your old reality, is through the affirmation process.

Saying your affirmations out loud first thing in the morning helps you to set up your day to be on the lookout for what you need.

Again, just before you go to sleep at night, repeat your affirmations out loud to help them sink into your subconscious as you sleep.

It's even better if you can repeat them several times throughout the day, too.

The affirmation (the words) gives you a vision (pictures) which triggers an emotion. Your emotion (reality) is stored in your subconscious. And who's the genius, who makes the outside reality match the inside reality?

Yes. You know it.

The more detailed, clear, and vivid the picture we give our subconscious, the easier it is for our subconscious to become creative and open our eyes to the hidden steps we need to achieve our goals.

You don't need to know how. The vision comes first. Let your subconscious figure out how. It's a genius.

It's like a guided missile; once it locks on, it locks out anything else.

You must think about what you DO want, not what you don't want. Your subconscious mind only deals with the subject matter, not whether or not you want it.

This is vital, and its why people with a "victim" mentality are always victims; they're always talking and thinking about the next bad thing that's going to happen to them. "Nothing good ever happens to me."

It's not because they're unlucky; it's because they constantly think about it and their subconscious just does what it's told.

See yourself in the future.

What does it look like when it's fixed?

Imagine yourself already there.

CHAPTER 17

BELIEF

For most of us, our belief in our own ability has developed over the years, just like our identity. It has become entrenched in who we are.

It's been created through our attempts at trying different things and how successful or unsuccessful we were. It's been reinforced by our teachers, our coaches, our parents.

Another word for belief is potential.

Up until this point, we have established our potential by what we believe we can achieve. How good we are, what we might achieve in life. But at the same time, we have also been putting a limit on it.

We have limited our potential at our belief level.

The problem with belief is this. Once you know (or think you know) what your limit is, that's as far as you can go. You cannot perform better than your potential (at least not consistently).

This potential becomes part of our identity. Yes, you're right: we can't do something we are not.

Sporting talent scouts travel all over the country looking for young athletes with potential. When they find them, they offer them scholarships and give them the best coaches to make the most of their potential. A good coach can raise your belief level, your potential to where they believe it can be. Is that the best it can be? No. They can still only raise it to their belief level, no further.

What is your true potential? Who knows?

When I was a teenager, I shot clay targets. I wasn't a bad shot, but I certainly wasn't a Russell Mark, either. I believed I was about a 9 out of 10 shooter; in a 10-target event, I would usually hit 9 of them.

If I missed a target early in the event, I would "dust" all of the rest, but if I was hitting them all early, I would start to get anxious and start thinking about missing a target. Inevitably, I would usually miss one.

I would self-regulate to my belief level. Potentially, maybe I could have gone to the Olympics with Russell Mark, but I never had the belief that I was good enough.

YOU MUST HAVE THE BELIEF TO MAKE SUSTAINABLE CHANGE.

Occasionally we perform above our belief level, above our potential, but as soon as that registers in our subconscious brain, we unknowingly sabotage ourselves.

To make any sustainable change in our lives, we must have the belief that it is possible. You must be able to see yourself doing it. Place yourself in your vision.

Belief

You're probably not going to get there on the first attempt. We rarely do, but we try again. If we fail again, we keep trying. When you have the belief, you will keep trying until you succeed.

A bloke called Thomas Edison believed he could make an electric light globe. He had the belief, and even though he failed thousands of times, eventually he made an electric light globe.

I can't imagine how good his self-talk must have been to keep re-affirming his belief. I'm not sure of his exact quote, but he defined the phrase "failure is not failure; it's just another way to not do it."

So, the point here is to not beat yourself up if you don't get it right the first time. Or the second time. Or the third, fourth, or thousandth. Beating yourself up is not going to do your self-esteem any favours.

You may need to re-affirm your belief to yourself to give you the energy and creativity you need to try again.

First comes the belief, then comes the trying, and then comes the reward.

Aaron Fotheringham is a young man with spina bifida who became the first person in the world to pull off a backflip in a wheelchair. A feat no one else believed possible. Not satisfied with that, he set his sights even higher and became the first person to double backflip a wheelchair. He doesn't put limits on his potential.

He now tours the world with Nitro Circus and is sponsored by several companies, including a wheelchair manufacturer. Who in their wildest dreams ever thought you could make a living just by wheeling a wheelchair? Aaron Fotheringham… and he prefers to call it "hardcore sitting."

This same belief can prevent you from achieving your goals or making your meaningful and sustainable change. If you believe it's not possible, that belief will become part of your identity, part of your subconscious. You'll build scotomas to the solution.

Remember how our RAS filters the information we receive, how we think we see the truth and the self-fulfilling prophecy? The same goes for our belief. What we believe is possible (and what we believe is not possible) has a huge effect on our actions, performance, abilities, and success.

Henry Ford once said, "Whether you believe you can do a thing or not, you are right."

Whatever your belief, you self-regulate your potential to it.

Its embedded in our subconscious, so as soon as our subconscious realises that we are performing above our potential, it takes control and restores our "normal." We lose concentration or we lose coordination. We start to question our ability. "This isn't like me." "I'm not usually this good, what's the matter?" Your negative self-talk takes over. Remember the old Cherokee Indian story. Subconsciously, you self-regulate back to your belief level.

We don't really know what our potential is, none of us. We actually have to grow into it. What I now know is that you have to have the belief first.

Oh, and by the way, it doesn't matter if no one else shares your belief.

Ever heard of a bloke called Christopher Columbus? Yeah? The only person in the world who believed the earth was round, not flat. Everyone thought he was crazy and laughed as he sailed his little boat out of the harbour, destined to fall off the end of the earth. When he returned triumphant, everyone believed.

It doesn't matter if you're the only person in the world who holds a belief; as long as you do, that's all that matters. Sometimes it might be a good idea to keep it to yourself so others won't try to "save" you from embarrassment.

YOU MUST SET YOUR GOAL. YOU MUST BELIEVE YOU CAN ACHIEVE IT AND LET YOURSELF GROW INTO YOUR POTENTIAL.

Don't feed the wrong wolf. All you need to do is say, "The next time I will be more like me, the next time I will… [say the words, visualise the goal, believe you will, feel the emotion, and then try again]." Affirm it to yourself.

While our belief is firmly embedded in us, we have the power to change it. Usually the way you do that is by visualisation, using your self-talk or the affirmation process.

So, what does that mean? You can do stuff you couldn't do before. You can do stuff you didn't believe you could do before. You can make the meaningful and sustainable change you couldn't make before.

Sometimes that change in belief can happen instantly, especially when combined with certain other circumstances.

If you make a vow, you know how powerful they are. I don't eat pumpkin.

If your vow is said at a special ceremony in front of your peers.

If your vow is validated by someone of authority.

A police cadet graduates from the academy, takes an oath (a vow) to uphold the law.

The chief of police presents him with his badge in front of the other cadets. Now he believes he's a policeman; he can arrest you. Before he was only a cadet; he couldn't.

A bride and groom walk into a church, believing they are single.

They say their vows in front of all their family and friends. "I do." The celebrant says, "I now declare you…"

They walk out believing they are married. Their actions and behaviours change in accordance with their new beliefs.

Now they can have sex. Before they couldn't.

Remember how our RAS works, how we think we see the truth?

Here's my question to you.

IF YOU BELIEVE IT'S NOT POSSIBLE.

IF YOU BELIEVE THERE IS NO SOLUTION TO YOUR PROBLEM.

COULD YOU BE BLOCKING THE SOLUTION?

CHAPTER 18
SELF-WORTH

What I know about self-worth or self-esteem is that you draw to yourself what you feel worthy of receiving. So, if in your mind, your self-appraisal is "I'm not worthy of that. I'm not good enough for that. That's too good for me," and opportunity comes your way, you subconsciously – not consciously – push it away. You don't even know you're doing it.

Let me tell you something right up front.

It's okay to know you're okay.

It's okay to feel worthy.

It's okay to have high self-esteem, high feelings of self-worth.

It's more than okay: I believe it's essential.

So, how do you build this high self-esteem?

AGAIN, WE'VE BUILT OUR OWN IMAGE, OUR OWN SELF-ESTEEM, WITH OUR OWN THOUGHTS.

It's become part of our identity, and we already know we can't do something we are not. In the same context, we can't receive anything better than our self-established self-worth.

Just like our identity, it's a DIY project, and it's a work in progress.

Right from a very young age, most of us have been taught to be humble or modest. Don't be a "big noter." We're taught to be gracious in victory. The meek shall inherit the earth and all that jazz.

It's all well and good to be humble and modest. It's all well and good to stand back and let others enjoy the spotlight. It's all well and good to acknowledge the contributions that others may have made towards your successes. OUTWARDLY.

Internally, though, you must allow your successes to become part of your identity. You must identify with being a winner, with being successful.

That's how successful people create their identity. That's how successful people establish their potential. That's how successful people build their self-esteem. That's how successful people become successful.

And that's exactly what you must do, too.

When someone gives you a compliment, don't shrug it off. All you need to do is simply say "thank you" out loud – but internally, to yourself, you must grab it with both hands, fist pump, and say, "YES!!!"

"I am good."

"I can achieve."

"I am a winner."

Self-Worth

Feel good about it and allow your subconscious to store it away in your identity. Allow your self-worth to grow with each and every compliment. Each and every success.

Because if you don't, it doesn't become part of you. If you say, "oh, it was nothing" or "I didn't have much to do with that," your subconscious accepts literally what you say. It doesn't store it in your memory (your reality). It's lost: the words are lost, the picture is lost, the emotion is lost.

You must allow yourself to feel the emotion of your accomplishments.

Those of you who have small children, here's an exercise for you to help them to develop good thinking patterns that will build their self-esteem and serve them well as adults. It's a good habit to get into yourself, too.

Each night when you tuck them into bed, ask them this question. "What did you do today that went really well for you?" Ask them how that made them feel. As they are retelling it, they are reliving it; remember I×V=R? This escalates their inner image of themselves.

Then what I want you to do is ask them, "And what are you looking forward to tomorrow?" What you are doing is taking their present positive emotion and dropping it into their visualisation of the future.

This is one of the qualities of every high-performance person in the world. They use what I call forethought to colour their future for tomorrow.

Let's go back and talk more about the power of compliments.

There are three levels of compliments.

The first level is "face-to-face compliments," where you simply give someone a compliment directly to them.

"Hey John, great presentation today, mate."

Now, if John has low self-esteem and doesn't know the value of accepting compliments, he can deflect this type of compliment quite easily. He's thinking, "Mary did all the hard work, she deserves the most praise" or "You're probably just saying that, you don't really mean it." He doesn't associate a positive emotion with it and he doesn't let it become part of his identity, part of his self-worth.

The next level is "third-party compliments." This is where you compliment someone by telling another person, in their company.

"Hey Mary, how good was John today giving that presentation?"

This time it's harder for John to deflect it, especially if Mary says, "Yeah, his contribution really made the difference." He's more likely to identify with the success, or at least part of it. He's more likely to feel good about it.

The third level I call "overheard compliments," where you're telling someone else and John accidentally overhears your conversation.

I'm on the phone talking to the boss: "Wow! Boss, you should've seen John's presentation today, he really smashed it." John overhears my phone conversation and thinks, "Mmmm, he really must think I'm good if he's telling the boss about it." He believes my compliment and allows himself to feel good about it, and it becomes part of his reality.

Parents, be aware of how you talk about your children when you're on the phone. You don't want to accidentally lock a negative identity into them if they overhear you.

"Billy's been a little shit today, he's so naughty." Billy will behave like it.

Learning how to accept compliments is one way to build your self-esteem. Getting into the habit of giving compliments is another.

By giving compliments to others, you are helping them to build their self-worth. How does that help you?

It's simple. It's the law of attraction. You get what you give. You attract what you are.

The more you compliment others, the better they feel about themselves and the better they feel about you. The more they want to be around you. You soon find yourself surrounded by people with high self-esteem. You feed off each other's energy.

Make it a habit – no, make it part of your identity to be a "complimenter," a payer of compliments. Find the good in others and tell them. It's amazing how much difference this one small thing can make to your life.

I tell people all the time how good they are. I compliment people I don't even know just to see the smile on their face.

Look for the good in people. Look for the positive. Let the media do the other.

So, if you're a complimenter and what you do is compliment people, what wouldn't you do?

You wouldn't be critical of people.

You wouldn't belittle people.

You wouldn't be sarcastic.

People who are sarcastic, who criticise, who belittle, are trying to devalue others. They're usually people with such low self-esteem and low self-worth themselves that instead of trying to build themselves up, they try to pull you down to their level.

They are trying to devalue your self-worth; don't let them. You have the power to accept or reject it.

Accept the complimentary.

Reject the belittling.

Ask them this question. "Are you saying that to make me feel bad about myself, or you feel better about yourself?"

If you find yourself constantly surrounded by these people, change your environment. Move away from them.

Don't let yourself do it to you, either.

You know every stupid thing you've ever done. You know every mistake you've ever made. Don't keep reminding yourself about how bad you felt.

Remember, I×V=R works just as well on your negative thoughts and your negative self-talk as it does on the positive.

Don't allow the negative stuff to take a stronghold in your reality, in your identity. Instead, turn it around: think about how you recovered from those setbacks. Think about how resilient you've become because of those mistakes. Think about the emotion you feel as you grow stronger. Make that strength part of your identity. Allow that to be your reality. Build up your self-esteem from your mistakes as well as from your successes.

So, when you do the next stupid thing, when you make the next mistake (and you will), remind yourself of how strong you are. Say to yourself, "I'm strong, I can do this. The next time I will be more like me, the next time I will… [say the words, visualise the goal, believe you will, feel the emotion, and then try again]." Affirm it to yourself.

Oh, and compliment yourself. When you are successful, give yourself a pat on the back. Tell yourself how good you are. The way most people are these days, if you're waiting around for someone else to tell you how good you are, you might be waiting a while.

You have to love yourself. More than that, you have to love yourself UNCONDITIONALLY.

I give myself compliments every day. I start when I'm shaving in the morning. I look in the mirror, give myself a wink, and in my best Joey Tribbiani voice I say, "how you doin'?"

I know that sounds a bit over the top. Try not to be overheard. I try to dress each day to make an impression, not just on myself but on other people. It's amazing how differently you're treated when you dress to impress. This might seem superficial, but I believe that to be successful, you need to first look like you're successful.

Don't be judgemental towards yourself, either. If you are, you'll find yourself at risk of identifying with that judgement. Then you know what happens once it becomes part of your identity.

There's one more thing that I've learned about self-worth.

When you receive what you feel worthy of, you must be thankful for it. You need to show gratitude. Be thankful to whoever it was that you received from. If you believe in God or a higher power, then show your gratitude to them also.

Yesterday Today Tomorrow

CHAPTER 19
COMFORT ZONES

A comfort zone is a place where you believe you belong, not necessarily where you're physically comfortable. A place where you feel safe emotionally. We all know what we're comfortable with and we all know what we're not, consciously. What we don't always realise is we have also established subconscious boundaries.

Guess who drew the boundaries of your comfort zones? Yep! You got it. You did.

It could be in a relationship, your career, socially, environmentally, recreationally – we've created comfort zones for ourselves everywhere.

Everybody knows where they feel comfortable socially. I know what kind of people I am comfortable being with.

If I find myself at the Ashes test at the Gabba and my seat is in the middle of the Barmy Army, I try to get out of it and get back to the familiar. Or, equally, if I find myself in the Members stand, I try to get out of it and get back to the familiar.

It's like when you ask your wife to come fishing with you.

Wife: "I'd love to come but I really wanted to reorganise the Tupperware cupboard today."

Me: "There'll be other wives there."

Wife: "It's okay, I really do need to have a day at home to catch up on the housework before Monday. Maybe if I'm not busy I'll come next time."

Her subconscious is at its creative best figuring out how to keep here in her comfort zone, anywhere but fishing.

Your comfort zone isn't always a "comfortable" place, though. Sometimes you just feel safe because you're too scared to go anywhere else.

Even though you're not happy there, you can't change it; you believe it's where you belong.

We have all tried to force ourselves out of a comfort zone with discipline, determination, or will-power. If you were tough enough, you stayed there, but most times that approach doesn't work.

We've all heard the clichés about how or why we need to get ourselves out of our comfort zones.

"Life begins at the end of your comfort zone."

"Great things never came from comfort zones."

"If you want to grow, you must step outside your comfort zone."

"Take the leap."

If you're brave enough to try, go for it. Chances are you're just going to get even more creative to go back to where you feel safe.

Fear is the number one reason why we don't get out of our comfortable zones or our uncomfortable places. Fear of the unknown. Fear and its two buddies, failure and regret.

We question ourselves. "What if I fail?" "What if I'm not good enough?"

I say, "What if you can do it without that fear?"

The old way we used to coach was a stupid way, but it was the only way we knew. We knew people had enormous potential, so we'd take them by the seat of the pants and throw them out there until they got used to it. We'd force them away from how good they thought they were and they'd grow into it.

You would make yourself get up there and give that talk. You would discipline yourself and force yourself out of your comfort zone. If you were tough enough to hang on, eventually your image would adjust.

But if you didn't, you'd feel embarrassed or ashamed. Your self-esteem would take a huge hit. You would be less likely to try again.

That's not the best way.

There's a better way.

The better way is: don't go there physically until you take yourself there safely in your mind. You need to talk yourself into it.

STRETCHING YOUR COMFORT ZONE IS A FAMILIARISATION PROJECT.

You need to visualise yourself going socially where you won't let yourself go.

Visualise yourself getting a job where you wouldn't let yourself get the job.

Visualise yourself on the podium at the Olympics.

You need to see yourself into the future and feel safe there.

THE ENEMY OF FEAR IS FAMILIARISATION.

Use your affirmations over and over and over until you become so familiar with your new environment, your fear is overwhelmed by the new emotion associated with your vision.

Make your desired zone more familiar than your comfort zone. We know why that's important.

When you're thrown out of your comfort zone, you block the input of information.

You subconsciously block the input of information. People can be talking to you, and you don't get the messages in. It's not because you're stupid, and not because you aren't capable. More than likely, it's because you're out of your comfort zone and you're focused on getting back into it.

When you're out of your comfort zone, your mind goes blank. It interferes with your recall and memory. You might be going for a test knowing the answers but once you get in to take the test, your mind goes blank. You can't remember. The minute you are out of the testing situation, the answer comes. It's the same with a job interview.

You could speak to a group of friends and relatives, but if you're asked to speak to 1000 strangers, you get in front of the group and immediately you're a deer in the headlights.

It's not about what you know; it's about what you can recall of what you know when in strange or unusual circumstances.

Your subconscious begins to sabotage you.

Comfort Zones

When you're out of your comfort zone, your upper body starts to constrict. You tighten up. You notice it in somebody's voice; it changes.

If you're a shooter and you're out of place, it affects your accuracy. It interferes with your fine motor skills. Your rib cage starts caving in on your lungs, making you out of breath.

People will say, "you know, I feel uptight about this." They're describing being out of their comfort zone, away from which, in their mind, they feel they belong.

"I feel uptight."

"I've been stupid; stay with the familiar."

"Go back where you belong."

"I've been under pressure lately."

Another thing that happens is your stomach secretes more digestive juice then you need. You start to get nauseated when you're out of place.

You are blocking information; you can't retrieve; your voice is changing on you; you're uptight; and now you're getting sick to your stomach. All of this happens when you try to force yourself away from your self-image.

All these describe the physiology striking you when you feel socially, environmentally, or personally out of place.

Now, you start to perspire. Moisture occurs immediately on the surface of your skin. That's how a lie detector works. They attach electrodes to the surface of your skin and ask a question they already know the answer to, so they get a register of the truth. Then they say, "were you at the crime scene?" "No." The needle goes off the scale.

You lose balance when you're out of your comfort zone.

What I now know is that when you're out of your comfort zone, it stimulates negative creativity. By negative, I mean avoidant. You get "avoid ideas." You get ideas about, "Why I should not go there. Why I can't do this. Why I can't do that. Why I should go back."

Go back to what? Go back to the familiar. Go back to where I'm safe. Go back to what I feel comfortable with. Go back to the way I'm supposed to be.

You start running down the future. You talk about why it's stupid, and why you don't want to go. That's creativity to keep you with your familiar, to keep you safe in your comfort zone. Your comfort zone becomes a prison around you.

People who actually do go to prison do hard time while they're first in prison. There's just turmoil inside of them. After about a year or so, they do easier time. You see, their system starts to adjust. They get comfortable with where they are.

Then, do you know what makes them upset? When they leave prison, they find it hard to leave. Some of them go out and commit a crime just so they can go back. They do it subconsciously. They don't know they're doing it.

It's called recidivism.

Ask yourself this question: "Where have I allowed myself to get comfortable?"

I work with people who have gone through a severe injury, and they get to a point where they don't want to leave their house. They don't want to leave the bedroom. They don't want to leave the hospital, let alone go after the opportunities that are out there.

They can't get themselves to do it.

It isn't like just going into the wrong bathroom. I've done that. I know where I belong. As long as I go to the right bathroom when I'm in public, I feel okay, I can use my potential.

I've gone into the women's room by mistake, not by intent. What goes on in my mind is, "how do I get out of here and get back to where I belong?"

I have the potential to use either room. It's just hard to use my potential when I'm in the wrong toilet.

Goal setting and stretching your comfort zone is a familiarisation project.

You need to familiarise yourself with the next step. You need to imagine yourself safely into the next environment, into the next situation.

It's a matter of taking yourself, in your mind, safely into the next level, into the next step.

You can't just do it once, though. You need to do it over and over and over. As you visualise yourself and stretch your comfort zone from where it has shrunk, as you visualise yourself into a new vocation, a new social world, a new lifestyle, the change you seek, then, you allow yourself to move into it.

Once I learned about comfort zones and visualisation, I let myself move into a new career.

I wasn't so afraid of public speaking, but I was terrified of charging money for it. There's no pressure speaking for free. It didn't matter if I didn't get good reviews. My future business didn't rely on me being good value for money. I had to picture myself delivering a speech worth the money.

I needed to practice in my mind so many things. I wouldn't force myself into it. I would just sit and practice.

ALL MEANINGFUL AND SUSTAINABLE CHANGE STARTS FIRST ON THE INSIDE, IN YOUR IMAGINATION.

You need to change your mind first. You sit and practice things going the way you want them to go. You practice in your imagination being who you want to be. You practice taking yourself into the new job, into the new world.

You practice making mistakes and learning from them, in your mind.

It must start in your mind.

You need to take yourself there safely in your mind first. You can't force yourself away.

It's not about willpower. That's the old way.

It isn't discipline. Discipline is forcing yourself away from your image. Forcing yourself out of your comfort zone.

This whole key is about taking yourself there comfortably. Expand your mind and place yourself into it, safely, comfortably.

CHAPTER 20
SELF-TALK

Your self-talk is the tool that you use to create:

Your IDENTITY

Your THOUGHT POWER

Your VISION

Your BELIEF

Your SELF-WORTH

Your COMFORT ZONES

Your OWNERSHIP

YOUR SELF-TALK IS THE CREATOR OF YOUR WORLD!

It's all about the way you talk to yourself!

It is absolutely vital that you choose the right words when you talk to yourself.

Listen to the way you talk to yourself.

Wow, if your friends talked to you the way you talk to yourself sometimes, well, they probably wouldn't be your friends any more.

Listen to your present self-talk and think about where it's taking you.

Ask yourself.

Is my self-talk taking me backwards?

Bruce Springsteen's song "Glory Days" typifies this type of self-talk. Some of us talk like our best days are in the past. They're not. They're yet to come.

Is my self-talk keeping me stuck where I am now?

You're describing your present situation to yourself, not the place you want to be. You're reinforcing it and making it even harder.

Is my self-talk moving me forward?

You're talking about what you do want, not what you don't want. You're describing what it looks like when it's fixed.

You could be your own fortune teller without needing a crystal ball. All you have to do is listen to your self-talk.

Are you talking about:

How things were.

How things are right now.

How things will be in the future.

Are you talking about:

What you do want.

Self-Talk

What you don't want.

I can't stress enough the importance of your self-talk and its role in achieving your meaningful and sustainable change.

It's the self-talk which gives us the pictures in our mind.

It's the pictures which give us the emotion.

It's the emotion that feeds our subconscious thoughts.

Remember what I said: you must use your self-talk to control your thoughts, or your thoughts will control you.

If you only remember one thing from reading this book, it should be this bit right here.

CONTROL YOUR SELF-TALK OR YOUR SELF-TALK WILL CONTROL YOU.

Why?

Because your subconscious does what you tell it.

Because not all self-talk is useful.

You see, there are four levels of self-talk.

The lowest level is called "negative resignation."

As the name suggests, this type of self-talk doesn't move you forward. Negative resignation is an impossibility statement, an inefficacious statement.

"I can't give up smoking."

"It's impossible to lose weight."

"There's no way I could…"

This level of self-talk will only move you backwards.

It's "victim mentality" self-talk.

"Nothing good ever happens to me."

This then becomes your reality.

Nothing good happens to you (or it does and you don't recognise it).

You don't give up smoking.

You don't lose weight.

More often than not, this type of self-talk moves you backwards.

Then there is "recognition" – the level where you know you have a problem, but you have no real intention to fix it. You want magic to fix it for you.

"I should give up smoking."

"I wish I could lose weight."

"I ought to…"

But if it's up to me, it's never going to happen.

This level of self-talk will only keep you where you are now. It's a bit like expecting to win lotto without buying a ticket. It's not going to happen.

Again, it's another inefficacious statement. It's not going to create change. You want someone else to change it for you.

You're waiting to win lotto.

The next level of self-talk is a "vow to change" – vows can work, especially if you are passionate about them.

"I don't smoke anymore."

"I'll never go there again."

"I don't eat pumpkin."

Have you ever said something like that? Everybody has something they've made a vow about. That can be the power of a vow. They're usually associated with a strong emotion.

The only problem with a vow is that it's usually about what you don't want to do, not what you do want to do.

Self-Talk

The highest level of self-talk and the level which you must reach is called "replacement pictures."

Another word for this type of self-talk is affirmation. Affirmations can create meaningful and sustainable change, especially if you use them repetitively and with emotion. They're about what you're going to do instead.

"I love the taste of breathing in fresh air."

"It feels great to be able to fit into my clothes again."

"I'm excited about being…"

"Replacement picture"-level self-talk or affirmations give you new goals. Why is that important?

YOU MUST HAVE A NEW GOAL OR YOUR SUBCONSCIOUS WILL DEFAULT BACK TO THE OLD ONE!

YOU HAVE GOT TO TALK ABOUT WHAT YOU DO WANT NOT WHAT YOU DON'T WANT!

There's a formula for writing effective affirmations.

Affirmations that will give you the pictures. As important as your self-talk is, its job is very simple. To give you the pictures.

Your affirmations need to:

- ☐ Be personal. It's about you (use "I" or "me") – you can't affirm for someone else.

- ☐ Be positive. It's got to be about what you DO want, not what you don't want.

- ☐ Be present tense. Like it's already happened.

- ☐ Indicate achievement. Use phrases like "I have," "I am," "I do." Avoid "I can," "I should," "I wish."

- ☐ Have no comparisons. It's your picture, not anyone else's; let them worry about their stuff.

- ☐ Use action words. Create a moving picture by using action words. "I rapidly…," "I easily…"
- ☐ Use emotion words. How do you want to feel? Use emotion words.
- ☐ Contain accuracy. It's got to be specific and detailed enough to give you a clear picture. Remember the five senses.
- ☐ Contain balance. Does it fit in with your identity and your life balance? You might need a separate affirmation to change your identity first.
- ☐ Be realistic. In the sense that you can see yourself achieving it. Only you know what you believe is realistic.
- ☐ Be confidential. Be particular with who you share your affirmations with. Will they be supportive?

The best affirmations tick all of these boxes.

Once you have written your affirmation or affirmations (it's probably best to start with just one or two until you become an "affirmer"), then you must use them as often as you can. Make it a part of your daily routine when you wake up in the morning and before you go to bed at night.

READ THE WORDS

SEE THE PICTURE

FEEL THE EMOTION

REPEAT

READ THE WORDS

SEE THE PICTURE

FEEL THE EMOTION

Sounds easy, right?

If it was easy, everybody would be doing it. Everybody would have everything they desired.

Self-Talk

It's not a complicated process, but it's not as easy as it sounds, especially if you're new to the process.

It's a two-part process.

1. Write an effective affirmation.

2. Repeat your affirmation, over and over and over and over and over and over...and over again.

Repetition is the key. Repetition changes short-term memory into long-term memory. Repetition changes conscious thoughts into subconscious thoughts.

That's where the power comes from. It can change your default settings.

I read a study that claimed:

A message read/heard only once is 66 percent forgotten in 24 hrs. It is less than 10 percent retained after 30 days.

A message read several times a day for eight days is virtually memorised, and almost 90 percent retained after 30 days.

Repetitious affirmations open up your subconscious to show you the way.

I use the affirmation process over and over and over.

I SAY THE WORDS.

I SEE THE PICTURE.

I FEEL THE EMOTION.

Using the affirmation process is the best way to change your thought patterns and change your life.

Every night before I go to sleep, I affirm to myself what my future looks like and I feel the emotion.

Every night I reflect on my day and ask myself the question: what was the highlight of my day? I relive it and reinforce it in my mind.

While I'm still feeling that emotion, I repeat my affirmations and ask myself: and what am I looking forward to tomorrow?

I take my emotion from today and I project it into tomorrow.

And the next day I go out and I find it. I tell myself what my day is going to be like the night before. It's a self-fulfilling prophecy.

You can talk yourself into doing anything you want to – anything at all.

Another way we use our self-talk is when we make a promise to ourselves.

When we make a promise to someone else, we usually keep it. If you give someone your word and you break it, you lose their respect. Your integrity is diminished. We go to great lengths to honour our word.

Why is it that we don't hold ourselves to the same level of accountability when we give our word to ourselves?

Are we less worthy of it? No. We're more worthy of it.

Keep your word when you give it to yourself, not just when you give it to others.

CHAPTER 21
OWNERSHIP

Motivation to make meaningful and sustainable change can come in many forms. It can come from within, or it can come from an outside source.

It can be an ultimatum: "do it, or else."

Or it can be your own free choice: "I choose to."

Yes, sometimes we all need to consider the wishes of others, but we still must maintain the right of free will. The right to make our own choices.

With everything going on in the world today, there are a lot of external influences affecting us. But there are two things that we have total control over, all of us.

THE WAY WE THINK.

and

THE CHOICES WE MAKE.

You can live your life from here forward on a "have to, victim, poor me, there's nothing I can do about this" basis, or you can take on your future on a "happy, want to, choose to, take charge, it's my idea" basis.

It's all the same to your creative subconscious mind. It will do what you tell it to do. That's why it's never the "victim mentality" person's fault. They are so creative about finding something or someone else to blame for their situation.

They identify as a victim.

They don't take control of their thoughts.

They can't visualise their future, or they think about what they don't want, not what they do want.

They believe there is no solution.

They don't feel worthy of anything but failure.

They are trapped in their comfort zones.

Their self-talk is "negative resignation."

They don't take responsibility for their own future.

Here's the deal breaker.

If you want to make meaningful and sustainable change in your life from this point forward…

IT'S GOT TO BE YOUR IDEA!

You've ticked seven of the boxes.

1. You know who you are.
2. You know how your thoughts work.
3. You can visualise your future.

Ownership

4. You believe you can do it.
5. You feel worthy of it.
6. You know how to stretch your comfort zones.
7. You can talk effectively to yourself.

Unless it's your idea, unless the meaningful and sustainable change you are trying to achieve is your idea, it's not going to happen.

As soon as the change becomes an ultimatum, a "have to or else"... It's called coercion. And guess who is the arch-enemy of coercion? Yep. You've got it. Your subconscious.

As soon as it's a "have to or else" situation, as soon as coercion is involved, then you're going to resist it with everything you've got, both consciously and subconsciously.

You are going to push back so hard. You're likely going to move in the opposite direction, away from the goal, if it's not your idea.

Now, when I say "your idea," it could be someone else's idea but you agree with it. You give sanction to it, and then it becomes your idea, too.

You know how it is when it's not your idea, though, when someone else tries to tell you what to do and what will happen if you don't?

You "have to" give up smoking, "or else" you'll get lung cancer and die.

"Is that so? Well, I'm just going to sit down and have a cigarette while I think about that. You know what? I might just have two. How do you like them apples?"

You know the coercion doesn't even have to come from someone else.

It doesn't have to come from outside.

It can come from within.

You could be trying to talk yourself into something that you really don't want to do and your other voice joins in.

"I'm going to the pub tonight, but I'm not going to have a cigarette."

"Yeah, right! Like that's likely to happen."

You'll do what the strongest voice tells you to do.

You could be trying to move away from your identity. You must be true to who you are.

You could be trying to throw yourself out of your comfort zone and rely on willpower alone.

Maybe it's something you're trying to do to please someone else – your partner, your family, your boss – and you're doing it for them, not for you.

It's got to be your idea.

It's all about free will.

It's all about choice. It's all about your choice.

It might be about whether or not you choose to use these eight keys.

The choice is yours.

Use them, don't use them – it's up to you.

I choose to use them and they work for me. They're not for everybody.

But if you do choose to use them, then give sanction to them and make them your idea, too.

They're my gift to you.

I don't know if they'll work for you.

All I know is they work for me.

Whatever you choose to do, I do encourage you to be the kind of human being who will take ownership of everything you can from here forward.

In whatever you do, take ownership of it. Make it your idea. Do it on an "It's my idea" basis.

It's up to you.

Only you can change your world.

Col Mackereth

Mentor - Author - Speaker

col@8keys.com.au

8Keys

www.8keys.com.au

www.ingramcontent.com/pod-product-compliance
Lightning Source LLC
Chambersburg PA
CBHW032036290426
44110CB00012B/833